Palgrave Studies in African Leadership

Series Editors

Faith Ngunjiri, Global Leadership Development LLC,
Windham, NH, USA
Nceku Nyathi, Royal Holloway University of London,
Egham, UK

Almost every continent has solid representation in the field of leadership studies except for Africa, despite its rapid growth. A groundbreaking series, Palgrave Studies in African Leadership fills a gap in the production of knowledge and scholarly publishing on Africa and provides a much needed outlet for the works of scholars interested in African leadership studies around the world. Where many studies of leadership in Africa focus solely on one country or region, this series looks to address leadership in each of the different regions and countries of the continent. This comes at a time when business and academic discourse have begun to focus on the emerging markets across Africa. The wide-ranging scholarly perspectives offered in this series allow for greater understanding of the foundation of African leadership and its implications for the future. Topics and contributors will come from various backgrounds to fully explore African leadership and the implications for business, including scholars from business and management, history, political science, gender studies, sociology, religious studies, and African studies. The series will analyze a variety of topics including African political leadership, women's leadership, religious leadership, servant leadership, specific regions, specific countries, specific gender categories, specific business entities in Africa, and more.

David Kelvin Amoo-Osae, Jr

Self-Protective Leadership and Organizational Effectiveness

Exploring a New Organizational Model for African Start-Ups

palgrave macmillan

David Kelvin Amoo-Osae, Jr
Accra, Ghana

ISSN 2945-6673 ISSN 2945-6681 (electronic)
Palgrave Studies in African Leadership
ISBN 978-3-031-61307-4 ISBN 978-3-031-61308-1 (eBook)
https://doi.org/10.1007/978-3-031-61308-1

This Palgrave Macmillan imprint is published by the registered company Springer Nature Switzerland AG
The registered company address is: Gewerbestrasse 11, 6330 Cham, Switzerland

To my dearest wife Annie and our cherished children—Wilma, Nate, Reuel, and Ann-Joelle:

You are the heartbeat of my existence, the guiding lights that illuminate my path. With every word penned in these pages, know that they are infused with the love and gratitude I hold for each of you. Annie, your unwavering support and boundless love have been my inspiration. Wilma, Nate, Reuel, and Ann-Joelle, your laughter and joy fuel my spirit, reminding me of the beauty that surrounds us.

In dedicating this work to you, I hope to honor the immeasurable impact you've had on my life. May these words serve as a testament to the love, strength, and unity that bind us together as a family.

With all my love,
David

Foreword

Through the decades, researchers worldwide have tried to ascertain the principal types of leadership and the conditions under which they enhance organizational effectiveness. In the contexts of the African start-up in Ghana and Kenya, Dr. Amoo-Osae Jr. posits a powerful thesis: that the various dimensions of self-protective leadership are critical drivers of start-up effectiveness under specific conditions of strategic entrepreneurial behavior. Drawing on survey and interview data, he uncovers significant variations in the effects of different dimensions of self-protective leadership.

I like the central argument in the book: knowledge of cultural and contextual factors is essential in understanding the dynamic role of self-protective leadership in start-up effectiveness. Supporting this argument, Amoo-Osae Jr. shows that procedural, self-centeredness, and conflict-induing leadership behaviors have divergent effects across start-ups in the two countries. Even more interesting is the finding that strategic entrepreneurial behavior plays a more critical moderating role in the relationship between self-protective leadership and start-up effectiveness in Ghana than in Kenya.

This book is profound in the theory of leadership. Still, luckily, Amoo-Osae Jr presents the theory in such a manner that it is accessible to both academics and managers. More importantly, he cleverly walks the reader through each book section with clearly defined guideposts to help the reader understand each chapter. He is meticulous in discussing the practical implications of the findings, offering valuable lessons to managers of start-ups, lessons that may also be useful for other firms outside the start-up environment.

Leadership promises the long-term development of national economies and success for companies, governments, and other African organizations threatened by volatile and ambiguous local and global environmental conditions. With the central thesis about self-protective leadership and findings from this rigorous study, Dr. Amoo-Osae Jr. has opened a new domain for leadership discourse, research, and managerial applications in Africa and worldwide. This book is insightful for all researchers and managers struggling to understand leadership in Africa. It provides refreshing insights to those serious about self-examining their leadership styles to counter deeply ingrained leadership ideas gained from the Western context.

When I set up the Nobel International Business School (NiBS) in 2014, I envisaged a school designed for executives to examine prevailing business and management practices in Africa to discover what works and does not work, to challenge their theory and practices to uncover new logics for managing and leading in the African context. We want executives to perform rigorous research to discover, lead, and share new ideas and practices. This book is a classic example of our ethos—Be Treasured: Discover. Lead. Share.

Prof. Kwaku Atuahene-Gima
Founder & President, Nobel
International Business School
(NiBS), Distinguished Professor
of Marketing & Innovation
Management
Accra, Ghana

Preface

Writing this book has been a profound journey, one that mirrors the many challenges and triumphs I have encountered throughout my professional and personal life. Reflecting on the path that has led me here, I am reminded of the pivotal moments and invaluable lessons that have shaped my understanding of leadership and entrepreneurship.

My motivations for writing this book stem from a deep-seated desire to share the knowledge and insights I have gained from my experiences in academia and the business world. This book targets a diverse audience, including aspiring entrepreneurs, business leaders, MBA students, and academics. It provides a comprehensive guide grounded in academic theory and real-world practice, offering a balanced perspective that is both insightful and practical.

Growing up in a well-off family, I witnessed firsthand the complexities of managing a successful business. My father, a prominent figure in our community, instilled in me the importance of diligence, strategic thinking, and the relentless pursuit of excellence. These early lessons became the foundation upon which I built my career.

However, life took a drastic turn during the political upheavals in Ghana. My family went from living in a large, comfortable home to starting from scratch. This transition from wealth to poverty and the struggle to rebuild our lives profoundly impacted me. It was during this challenging period that I developed a keen eye for opportunities and a relentless drive to succeed.

As I ventured into the business world, I was struck by the high failure rates of start-ups, particularly in the African business context and terrain. This observation fueled my curiosity and led me to delve deeper into the reasons behind these failures. Through extensive research and practical experience, I discovered that the unique challenges faced by African entrepreneurs required a tailored approach to leadership and business management.

The concept of self-protective leadership, central to this book, emerged from exploring these challenges. Self-protective leadership emphasizes the need for business leaders to prioritize their interests while navigating the complex dynamics of their organizations. It is a leadership style that acknowledges the realities of our business environment, where trust is a scarce commodity and the stakes are incredibly high. I learned early on that in business; you must protect your investment and interests because employees and partners might not always share the same level of commitment.

One of the core themes of this book is the importance of strategic and entrepreneurial behavior in ensuring the success and sustainability of a business. Through my journey—from the inception of my first business ventures to the establishment of successful enterprises like Movie House Plaza—I have learned that adaptability, continuous learning, and a keen understanding of market dynamics are crucial for long-term success. For instance, my background in marketing and advertising allowed me to innovate and create a unique business model that catered to high-end private movie screenings, eventually dominating the market.

This book is also a testament to the power of mentorship and the impact of influential figures in our lives. Throughout my career, I have been fortunate to learn from exceptional leaders and mentors who have guided me, challenged me, and inspired me to reach new heights. Their wisdom and support have been instrumental in shaping my leadership philosophy, and I am deeply grateful for their contributions. Leaders, like my former CEO, who demonstrated charismatic and competent leadership, and my academic mentors, who opened my eyes to the intricate theories and practices of effective leadership, have all played a significant role in my development.

To my readers, I hope this book serves as a valuable resource and a source of inspiration. Whether you are an entrepreneur embarking on a new venture, a business leader seeking to refine your strategies, or a student eager to understand the intricacies of effective leadership, I believe the insights shared in these pages will resonate with you.

As you read through the chapters, you will find a blend of personal anecdotes, case studies, and practical advice designed to equip you with the tools and knowledge necessary to navigate the challenges of the business world. I aim to empower you to make informed decisions, foster innovation, and ultimately succeed in your endeavors.

This book is the first in a series to explore different aspects of business development and leadership. The subsequent volumes will delve into medium to long-term strategies for sustaining and growing a business, ensuring that you are well-equipped to face the evolving challenges of the business landscape.

Thank you for joining me on this journey. I am excited to share my experiences and insights with you, and I look forward to the positive impact this book will have on your personal, academic, and professional growth.

With gratitude,

Accra, Ghana

Dr. David Kelvin Amoo-Osae, Jr

Acknowledgments

This book is in many respects inspired by the BIG SIX (6) GENTLEMEN who made me who and what I am today.

First, the Late Mr. David Amoo-Osae Sr. (Building Contractor & Partner, Arrow Construction Works). I came from his loins, and he breathed life into me, strongly determining the foundation and direction for my life. It was always his way or the highway. It now makes sense.

Second, the Late Brigadier-General (Rtd) Dr. Daniel Ampadu-Twum (Former Commanding Officer of the 37 Military Hospital), who taught me how to be a shrewd businessman as well as all the "good and bad" things one needs to be fully grounded as a strong man, father, husband, and leader.

Third, the Late Mr. Daniel Ampadu-Twum Jr. (Founder of the Unicorn Group & CEO of Origin8 Saatchi & Saatchi), who gave me my first job with the most informal interview ever and showed me the importance of exemplary leadership and self-belief while keeping your eye on the ball (money and profits).

Fourth, Mr. Emmanuel T. Obeng (CEO of Digitronix Ltd and Jishlah Financial Services Ltd), who taught me the fine details of moving from a start-up business to becoming a known and respected brand nationwide and beyond successfully.

Fifth, Prof. Atuahene-Gima (Founder and Executive Dean of Nobel International Business School—NiBS), who introduced me to executive education and the remodeling of my academic and practice mindset with two world-class institutions, changing my executive learning and business life forever: China Europe International Business School (CEIBS)—Executive Master of Business Administration (EMBA), and SBS Business School/Nobel International Business School (NiBS)—Doctor of Business Leadership (DBA).

Finally, Mr. Joel E. Nettey (CEO of Ninani Group & Immediate Past World President & Chairman at International Advertising Association), who taught me the very rudiments of everything I know about marketing communications client service/management, as well as the unstoppable belief that with determination and preparation, everything is possible. Even the word IMPOSSIBLE has POSSIBLE in it.

One day. One day very soon.
To God be the glory. Amen!

Praise for *Self-Protective Leadership and Organizational Effectiveness*

"Dive into a riveting exploration where traditional leadership meets entrepreneurial spirit! This book fearlessly challenges conventional wisdom, offering a refreshing perspective on transforming startups in Africa and beyond. Ready to rethink your approach? Embark on this phenomenal journey and unlock the secrets to success in business, defying stereotypes along the way."

—Hod Anyigba, Ph.D., *Executive Director, Africa Labour Research and Education Institute (ALREI), Chief Economist, International Trade Union Congress (ITUC)-Africa, Managing Partner, Innolead International Ghana*

"David Amoo Osae's book on leadership and organisational effectiveness represents groundbreaking work on issues attendant to how entrepreneurs navigate the complexities of business using a novel self-protective leadership philosophy. This book is highly recommended."

—Professor Robert E. Hinson, *Pro Vice Chancellor, Ghana Communication Technology University, Faculty (Marketing & Entrepreneurship), University of Ghana Business School, International Marketing Scholar & Strategist*

"This book examines the relationship between self-protective leadership (SPL) and organizational effectiveness of African start-ups. This is really an interesting piece, based on an empirical study. It signals major differences in the effects of various SPL dimensions on start-up effectiveness across countries. The book provides important managerial implications and will be a valuable resource for business leaders, researchers, and students. I strongly recommend it."

—Professor Joshua Yindenaba Abor, *Professor of Finance and former Dean, University of Ghana Business School*

"This book explores a unique leadership style, Self-Protective Leadership (SPL), from an African perspective for African start-ups. Through in-depth analysis, the book unpacks how cultural factors and strategic behaviour impact leadership. Coming from a business setting where documentation of learnings from both experience and observation is a challenge, this insightful study offers valuable guidance for both leadership development and organizational strategy in Africa's dynamic entrepreneurial landscape."

—Mr. Joel Edmund Nettey, *Imm-Past World President & Chairman, International Advertising Association (IAA), CEO, The Ninani Group*

"In this thought-provoking research on Self-Protective Leadership (SPL) and Organizational Effectiveness in African Start-Ups, Dr. David Amoo-Osae, Jr. reshapes leadership paradigms. He underscores the significance of SPL in fostering organizational resilience, having conducted empirical studies in Ghana and Kenya.

Dr. Amoo-Osae Jr's findings promote SPL as an approach that fosters team spirit and productive well-being, providing leaders with a road map for navigating challenging environments. Explore this novel research that guides a vibrant African entrepreneurship future."

—Dr. Humphrey Ayim-Dake, *President, Association of Ghana Industries., Chairman, RedMoon Resources Ltd.*

"Self-protective leadership encourages a proactive approach to risk management. Entrepreneurs can minimize the impact of unforeseen challenges and maintain the resilience of their businesses. By embracing the principles of resilience, adaptability, and strategic foresight, entrepreneurs can safeguard their ventures against risks while fostering innovation and growth especially in doing business in Africa. I wholeheartedly endorse this book and encourage fellow business leaders to embrace this approach in their entrepreneurial endeavors."

—Dr. Tracey Clark Jeffries, *University of Missouri, St. Louis, CEO, Capital Consulting Services, USA*

"Overcoming the liability of newness and fostering strategic behaviour is crucial for start-up businesses. This tremendous scholarly work lays out the cultural dynamics and unique impact of the self-protective Leadership (SPL) style on the African business terrain. SEB, as a moderator, changes the perceived negativity of the SPL style into a positive one for Africans doing business in Africa. Africa finally has its leadership theory!"

—Dr. Moses Tiffa Baio (LLB, MBA, DBL), *Director of Presidential Infrastructure Delivery Unit (Office of the President of the Republic of Sierra Leone,)Former Director General, Sierra Leone Civil Aviation Authority*

"This book is a valuable resource for leadership development and organizational strategy for startups and small businesses in Africa. It identifies gaps in contemporary literature on self-protective leadership's impact on effectiveness. The author highlights the importance of understanding socio-cultural and economic contexts, revealing limitations in current leadership theories.

I endorse the book as a treasured resource in leadership development, business strategy and policy formulation for startups and SMEs in Africa."

—Dr. Muda Yusuf, *Founder/CEO, Centre for the Promotion of Private Enterprise [CPPE], Nigeria*

"While there are numerous studies on entrepreneurship, perhaps none has been this pointedly focused on unique African perspectives on start-up leadership traits. New knowledge extends or challenges our understanding, and this book does just that.

It innovatively blends new theoretical frameworks with empirical findings and challenges conventional or Western wisdom in the subject area. It is indeed a playbook which provides priceless insights into overcoming startup challenges in Africa."

—Mr. Benjamin Mensah, *Executive Head, Personal & Private Banking, Stanbic Bank Ghana Ltd.*

"This groundbreaking scholarly work represents a paradigm shift in African business scholarship. With meticulous research and innovative insights, it unveils the transformative potential of strategic entrepreneurial behavior in navigating complex socio-cultural landscapes. A seminal contribution to leadership theory and practice, this work heralds a new era of strategic leadership in Africa and for African entrepreneurs. It is a must-read book for scholars and practitioners alike."

—Dr. Ing. Stephen Debrah-Ablormetti, *Managing Director, CPL Developers Ltd.*

"With practical insights based on science and data, it equips African entrepreneurs with the most appropriate leadership theory, i.e., Self-Protective Leadership style, coupled with Strategic Entrepreneurial Behaviour, to succeed in Africa's complex cultural-centric business landscape. A must-read for every entrepreneur in Africa's start-up business ecosystem. "

—Dr. Mrs. Annie Gervalice Amoo-Osae, *Executive Director, The House Group*

Contents

Abbreviations

AVE	Average Variance Extracted
BLT	Behavioral Leadership Theory
CFA	Confirmatory Factor Analysis
EFA	Exploratory Factor Analysis
GLOBE	Global Leadership and Organizational Behavior Effectiveness
SEB	Strategic Entrepreneurship Behavior
SLT	Situational Leadership Theory
SMEs	Small & Medium Enterprises
SPL	Self-Protective Leadership
SSA	Sub-Saharan Africa

1 Introduction

Abstract In today's fast-paced and unpredictable global business environment, leadership styles are crucial in shaping how organizations succeed. This book explores the often-overlooked concept of Self-Protective Leadership (SPL), particularly within African start-up businesses in Ghana and Kenya. Identified by the Global Leadership and Organizational Behavior Effectiveness (GLOBE) project, SPL is a leadership style common in regions with colonial histories.

1.1 Leadership in the Business World

In today's fast-paced and unpredictable global business environment, leadership styles are crucial in shaping how organizations succeed. This book explores the often-overlooked concept of Self-Protective Leadership (SPL), particularly within African start-up businesses in Ghana and Kenya. Identified by the Global Leadership and Organizational Behavior Effectiveness (GLOBE) project, SPL is a leadership style common in regions with colonial histories. It examines how SPL impacts the effectiveness of organizations (House et al., 2004).

D. K. Amoo-Osae, Jr, *Self-Protective Leadership and Organizational Effectiveness*, Palgrave Studies in African Leadership, https://doi.org/10.1007/978-3-031-61308-1_1

Leadership is more than just guiding a team to meet goals. It's about creating a vision, building a strong culture, and inspiring people to do their best work. In the world of African start-ups, leadership plays an even more critical role because of the unique challenges and opportunities that entrepreneurs face. Challenges like limited access to funding, infrastructure gaps, and fierce competition are common (Schoar, 2010). But there are also significant opportunities in untapped markets, innovation potential, and leveraging cultural strengths (Amankwah-Amoah, 2016).

Self-Protective Leadership shifts the focus from just influencing others to a balanced approach that includes taking care of the leader's well-being. This is especially important in Africa, where leaders often deal with additional stress from political instability and economic uncertainty (Zoogah, 2008).

In many African start-ups, leaders are usually the founders, meaning they not only have the vision for the business but also manage its daily operations. This dual role can be incredibly stressful, as the pressure to succeed and fear of failure are constant. SPL provides a framework that helps leaders manage this stress by prioritizing their well-being, building resilience, and maintaining a healthy work-life balance (Kompier & Cooper, 1999). By doing so, leaders can remain effective and motivate their teams to perform at their best.

For instance, take M-Pesa, the mobile money service that transformed financial transactions in Kenya. The leaders behind M-Pesa navigated a complex regulatory environment, secured funding, and built a robust technology platform. Throughout this journey, principles of SPL like resilience and proactive stress management were key to their success (Hughes & Weiss, 2007). Today, M-Pesa is not just a financial powerhouse in Kenya but also a model for other African start-ups (Jack & Suri, 2011).

1.2 Understanding Self-Protective Leadership

The self-protective leadership dimension stands out among various leadership styles due to its demonstrated effectiveness in safeguarding the survival of start-up enterprises. This leadership approach prioritizes the safety and security of both leaders and the group, encompassing traits such as self-centeredness, status-consciousness, conflict-inducement, face-saving, and procedural adherence (GLOBE Studies, 2006). Given that business owners typically steer the vision and financial course of their ventures, safeguarding the leader's interests becomes paramount. Consequently, employee involvement in business management tends to be minimal, with operations primarily directed toward protecting the leader's interests. The intricate dynamics inherent in self-protective leadership, particularly the concentration of leadership authority within a single individual, warrant scholarly investigation. Accordingly, this study aims to explore the influence of the self-protective leadership style on start-up enterprises in Africa.

While leadership research has a rich history, entrepreneurship research is increasingly gaining prominence as a fruitful area for scholarly exploration (Zach & Baldegger, 2017). This trend reflects the growing recognition that effective strategic entrepreneurship serves as a vital source of competitive advantage. The leadership style adopted by strategic entrepreneurs significantly influences organizational development, service quality, competitiveness, employee engagement, cost reduction, and pragmatism (Bamiatzi et al., 2015). For example, a strong leadership style combined with strategic entrepreneurship has been shown to enhance employee job satisfaction by aligning their interests with organizational goals, thereby motivating them to strive for and potentially surpass organizational and managerial objectives (Akbari et al., 2017). This evidence underscores the increasing integration of leadership and strategic entrepreneurship into the daily practices of Chief Executive Officers (CEOs) and management, recognizing them as pivotal factors in the success of new ventures (Batistič et al., 2017).

Research findings suggest a strong correlation between investor decisions and entrepreneurial effectiveness (MacMillan et al., 1985; Reid et al., 2018). Specifically, investors tend to select companies based on the perceived significance of leadership, particularly its influence on individual employees and overall company performance. Moreover, among the top ten factors influencing investor decisions, five are related to the entrepreneur's experience or personality (Ensley et al., 2006; McColl-Kennedy & Anderson, 2002). Given the distinct characteristics of start-up ventures compared to established businesses, understanding the context of start-up enterprises is crucial for investigating the moderating relationship between self-protective leadership and the success of start-up firms, particularly from the perspective of emerging economies.

Moreover, in current scholarship, there is a prevailing belief that businesses demonstrating entrepreneurial behaviors tend to outperform their conservatively managed counterparts, all else being equal (Rosenbusch et al., 2011). While numerous factors influence success, entrepreneurial behavior is widely recognized as a potent predictor of performance both within and across firms (Rauch et al., 2009). The literature on strategic entrepreneurship consistently supports the idea that being not just an entrepreneur but a strategic, creative, and responsive one yields dividends (Ireland et al., 2003). The central query now centers on how entrepreneurial creativity and responsiveness are actualized. To provide a satisfactory answer, scholars must delve into the construct of Strategic Entrepreneurial Behaviors (SEB).

The SEB framework encompasses a company's exploration of new markets, products, and opportunities through the deliberate commercialization of its product innovations or technologies. This framework delineates the requirements for a company to consistently exhibit a behavioral inclination toward engaging in product/market entrepreneurial endeavors. Strategic entrepreneurship behavior parallels a firm's entrepreneurial orientation, which encompasses its creative risk-taking behaviors, operational approach, and proactive mindset (Anderson et al., 2009; Covin & Slevin, 1991). However, SEBs isolate only the behavioral facets of a firm's strategic initiatives that specifically steer the firm into new product/market domains, distinguishing it from entrepreneurial orientation.

Start-up firms face two primary challenges commonly referred to as the "liabilities of newness." The first challenge involves establishing revenue streams and managing cost structures effectively by leveraging internal capabilities efficiently. The second challenge revolves around finding innovative approaches to address the rapid evolution of new technologies and the short lifespan of many technology products and services driven by intense industry competition (Tukker & Tischner, 2017). This situation underscores the need for ambidexterity in terms of creativity among start-up businesses, epitomized by the simultaneous balance of exploitation and exploration activities (Hughes et al., 2020; Simsek, 2009; Volery et al., 2015; Voss & Voss, 2013).

However, engaging in both exploitation and exploration activities concurrently may present challenges for organizations. Excessive focus on exploitation may lead the young firm to develop its capabilities rigidly, inhibiting its ability to innovate. Conversely, excessive exploration may risk the firm's sustainability, potentially trapping it in perpetual product/service development cycles with limited market success (Hughes, 2018). Strategic entrepreneurship emerges as a potential solution, representing the extent to which a firm integrates opportunity-seeking and advantage-building behaviors (Kuratko & Audretsch, 2013; Mazzei et al., 2017; Withers et al., 2018).

As previously mentioned, overcoming the liability of newness and fostering strategic entrepreneurial behavior are crucial for start-up businesses, including those within the marketing communication industry. Leadership emerges as a pivotal factor in this endeavor. Hence, this study investigates the impact of the self-protective leadership style on start-up enterprises in the marketing communication sector in Africa, specifically in Ghana and Kenya.

1.3 Bridging the Gap: SPL and African Start-Ups

This book aims to enrich existing scholarship in two significant ways. Firstly, it seeks to deepen the understanding of the concept of self-protective leadership within the broader context of business theorization. Secondly, it endeavors to conduct an empirical investigation into the African business landscape to elucidate the influence of self-protective leadership on start-up enterprises in Africa, with a focus on Ghana and Kenya. These articulated objectives stem from identified gaps in the current literature and are driven by the scholarly imperative to address these gaps. The study aims to shed light on some of the key deficiencies in existing literature that inspire the present research endeavor.

The Global Leadership and Organizational Behavior Effectiveness (GLOBE) report (GLOBE Studies, 2006) underscores the cultural influence on self-protective leadership, while Wanasika et al. (2011) assert that the paternalistic leadership prevalent in Sub-Saharan Africa (SSA) is deeply rooted in culture. The latter study highlights the recognition across SSA nations of the inhibitive nature of the "African strong man" leadership archetype. Consequently, there is a rejection of paternalistic organizational leadership in Africa. Despite the valuable cultural insights provided by these studies, there is a noticeable absence of research focusing on the specifics of the self-protective leadership style within the African business context. Additionally, there is a dearth of scholarship addressing the nuances and typology of the self-protective leadership style within the marketing communication industry in Africa.

The behavioral trends observed in start-ups within the African marketing communications industry warrant a critical examination of the leadership factors that underlie such patterns. For instance, it is common practice in the African industry for employees to depart and establish their own ventures after gaining experience in mainstream marketing communications firms. Many of these start-ups experience initial success within the first two to three years of operation, followed by a subsequent decline (Krause & Pullman, 2021; Lemley & McCreary, 2021). A significant proportion of these new ventures fail to sustain themselves beyond their fifth year of operation (Forde, 2021). This recurring pattern of behavior presents theoretical and leadership challenges that necessitate thorough investigation.

Given the afore-mentioned challenges, which remain insufficiently addressed in existing literature, the current study directs its attention toward leadership within the African marketing communications industry, with a particular emphasis on the start-up segment. Through this focused analysis, the study aims to enhance understanding of leadership theory and management practices while also integrating the underexplored African start-up sector into mainstream scholarly and leadership discussions. This endeavor seeks to contribute to the enrichment of existing scholarship and the advancement of knowledge in both leadership theory and African business contexts.

1.4 Significance and Contributions

This book holds significant importance for the scholarship on start-up leadership by proposing a model tailored for adoption by self-protective leaders within the African start-up context. By doing so, the study contributes to the development of empirically derived guiding principles toward a theory of business leadership in Africa. Drawing from Mangaliso's (2001) observations, which highlight the disparity between Western management theories and the African socio-cultural, political, and economic context, it becomes evident that theories crafted by Western scholars may not seamlessly align with the African landscape. Therefore, the present research assumes paramount importance within African business and intellectual spheres. It offers an African solution rooted in the empirical examination of African business challenges aimed at enhancing the effectiveness of African businesses.

Indeed, the significance of the study extends beyond the African context as the leadership model it proposes enriches the perspectives of leadership practitioners, policymakers, labor experts, scholars, and thought leaders globally. By introducing an African leadership paradigm into the discourse, the study diversifies and broadens the landscape of leadership theories, which have historically been dominated by Western voices. This paradigm shift not only acknowledges the unique challenges and dynamics of leadership in Africa but also contributes to a more inclusive and comprehensive understanding of leadership principles worldwide. Thus, the study's impact resonates across borders, fostering a more holistic approach to leadership theory and practice.

The contribution of the book is multifaceted. Firstly, it identifies significant opportunities for leadership scholars to leverage theoretical advancements derived from the self-protective leadership literature. By utilizing the five dimensions of the self-protective leadership style—self-centeredness, status-consciousness, conflict-inducement, face-saving acts, and procedure-orientedness—as outlined in the GLOBE Studies (2006), the study serves as a catalyst for identifying new avenues to advance the concept of the self-protective leadership approach. It is important to note that while recognizing the value of other leadership styles, this research focuses specifically on the self-protective leadership approach. Overall, this study offers a pioneering evaluation of the intersection between self-protective leadership and start-up enterprises, filling a critical gap in the existing literature on the topic.

Secondly, the study sheds light on the sub-constructs within self-protective leadership and strategic entrepreneurship behavior, drawing from the proposed dimensions outlined by the GLOBE Studies (2006). Through a comprehensive synthesis of existing literature, the research evaluates the progress and ongoing debates in the field. Guided by critical perspectives, the study poses two fundamental questions: first, examining the impact of self-protective leadership dimensions on start-up businesses, and second, exploring how strategic entrepreneurship behavior influences the relationship between self-protective leadership dimensions and start-up enterprises. Additionally, the study extends the framework of self-protective leadership dimensions introduced by the GLOBE Studies (2006) by employing a sequential explanatory research method to refine the original instruments. Consequently, the research endeavors to conceptualize an African model of the self-protective leadership style tailored specifically for the continent's start-up business sector.

Thirdly, this research aims to offer guidance and solutions to address the leadership gap prevalent in start-up businesses across Africa. By delving into the relatively unexplored territory of the self-protective leadership style and its associated traits, the study stands to make a significant contribution to the literature. Indeed, there is a notable scarcity of data and research on this topic, particularly within the context of African start-up enterprises. Recognizing the pivotal role of start-ups in bolstering Sub-Saharan African economies by providing essential support in terms of employment and tax revenue, the success of these ventures holds immense importance. Therefore, the outcomes of this research, if successful, promise to enrich existing knowledge on the strategies necessary for start-up businesses to navigate through the initial challenges and thrive in the business ecosystem.

Fourth and finally, the justification for situating the present research within the African context is twofold. Firstly, the self-protective leadership style stands out as the sole African leadership theory available, uniquely rooted in typical African cultural ethos. Unlike other leadership styles, this approach emphasizes the grooming and shaping of African leaders to endure and thrive during the critical initial three to five years of business establishment. It equips African leaders with the requisite skills and understanding necessary for navigating the challenges inherent in start-up ventures within the African landscape. Secondly, by offering nuanced insights derived from empirical research, this study aims to further enrich the knowledge base of African business practitioners. It empowers them with the tools and understanding needed to successfully establish and sustain new businesses in Africa, thus enabling them to navigate through the complexities and uncertainties of the entrepreneurial journey.

1.5 Key Concepts and Definitions

Certain words and terms are frequently used throughout this book. To enhance understanding and clarity of the same within the book's context, a thorough glossary of definitions is included below.

Leader: An individual capable of influencing a group of people towards achieving a common goal (Northouse, 2007).
Leadership: The practice of inspiring a group of individuals to collaborate towards a shared objective (Daft, 2005).
Self-Protective Leadership: A leadership approach focused on bolstering status and preserving face to ensure individual and group protection and security (GLOBE Studies, 2006).
Self-Centered: Pertaining solely to one's own desires, needs, or interests (GLOBE Studies, 2006).

Self-Conscious: Involving a state of nervousness or discomfort due to anxiety about others' perceptions of one's personality and actions (GLOBE Studies, 2006).
Conflict Inducer: Reflecting a desire to foster rivalry within a community, possibly through secrecy about information and a refusal to collaborate with others (GLOBE Studies, 2006).
Face-Saving: Ensuring that followers are not humiliated or shamed, maintaining positive relationships by refraining from negative feedback, and utilizing metaphors and examples (GLOBE Studies, 2006).
Procedural: Pertaining to the adherence to established standards, laws, policies, procedures, and daily routines (GLOBE Studies, 2006).
Strategic Entrepreneurial Behavior: Involves a company's utilization of emerging consumer markets by commercializing its product developments or technologies (Anderson et al., 2019).
Liability of Newness: Refers to the challenge faced by new organizations in competing successfully against existing ones (Stinchcombe, 1965).

1.6 Organization of the Book

This book is structured to provide a comprehensive exploration of self-protective leadership (SPL) within the context of African business environments, delving into its definitions, dimensions, historical contexts, implications for organizational effectiveness, and its role in the globalized economy.

This introductory chapter has set the stage for understanding self-protective leadership by providing an overview of its significance in contemporary leadership discourse. It has outlined the key objectives of the book, introduced fundamental concepts, and established the framework for subsequent discussions.

Chapter 2 delves into the core concepts of self-protective leadership, offering a detailed definition, elucidating its scope, and identifying its various dimensions. By establishing a clear understanding of SPL, this chapter lays the groundwork for exploring its applications and implications in subsequent chapters. It serves as a foundation, ensuring that readers are well-versed in the essential elements of SPL before moving on to more complex discussions.

Chapter 3 examines the historical and institutional contexts of leadership development in Africa. It traces the evolution of leadership paradigms within the continent and highlights cultural, political, and socio-economic factors that have shaped leadership practices. Understanding these contexts is crucial for contextualizing SPL within African business landscapes, providing a comprehensive backdrop against which SPL can be analyzed and understood.

Chapter 4 explores different models of organizational leadership behavior, providing a theoretical framework for understanding leadership dynamics within businesses. By examining various theoretical perspectives, this chapter enriches the reader's understanding of leadership approaches and sets the stage for evaluating SPL within organizational contexts. It bridges the gap between theoretical concepts and practical applications, enhancing the overall comprehension of leadership behavior.

In Chapter 5, the book investigates the relationship between self-protective leadership and organizational effectiveness through empirical research and case studies. By analyzing the impact of SPL on organizational outcomes, it offers valuable insights into the dynamics of leadership effectiveness in African business settings. This chapter provides concrete examples and data-driven analysis, illustrating the practical implications of SPL in real-world scenarios.

The concluding chapter reflects on the future prospects of self-protective leadership in the globalized economy alongside conclusions and recommendations specifically tailored for start-up businesses. It delves into emerging trends, challenges, and opportunities pertinent to SPL adoption and adaptation across varied cultural and economic settings, presenting invaluable insights for leaders as they navigate the intricacies of our interconnected world.

References

Akbari, M., Amiri, N. S., Imani, S., Rezaeei, N., & Foroudi, P. (2017). Why Leadership Style Matters: A Closer Look at Transformational Leadership and Internal Marketing. *The Bottom Line, 30*(4), 258–278.

Amankwah-Amoah, J. (2016). Global Business and Emerging Economies: Toward a New Perspective on the Effects of E-commerce on the Global Economy. *Journal of World Business, 51*(4), 548–559.

Anderson, B. S., Covin, J. G., & Slevin, D. P. (2009). Understanding the Relationship Between Entrepreneurial Orientation and Strategic Learning Capability: An Empirical Investigation. *Strategic Entrepreneurship Journal, 3*(3), 218–240.

Anderson, B. S., Eshima, Y., & Hornsby, J. S. (2019). Strategic Entrepreneurial Behaviors: Construct and Scale Development. *Strategic Entrepreneurship Journal, 13*(2), 199–220.

Bamiatzi, V., Jones, S., Mitchelmore, S., & Nikolopoulos, K. (2015). The Role of Competencies in Shaping the Leadership Style of Female Entrepreneurs: The Case of North West of England, Yorkshire, and North Wales. *Journal of Small Business Management, 53*(3), 627–644.

Batistič, S., Černe, M., & Vogel, B. (2017). Just How Multi-Level is Leadership Research? A Document Co-citation Analysis, 1980–2013 on Leadership Constructs and Outcomes. *The Leadership Quarterly, 28*(1), 86–103.

Covin, J. G., & Slevin, D. P. (1991). A Conceptual Model of Entrepreneurship as Firm Behavior. *Entrepreneurship Theory and Practice, 16*(1), 7–26.

Daft, R. L. (2005). *The Leadership Experience* (3rd ed.). Thomson South-Western.

Ensley, M. D., Hmieleski, K. M., & Pearce, C. L. (2006). The Importance of Vertical and Shared Leadership within New Venture Top Management Teams: Implications for the Performance of Startups. *The Leadership Quarterly, 17*(3), 217–231.

Forde, W. (2021). Strategies to Improve the Survival Rate Beyond 5 Years for Small Business in Guyana (PhD Thesis).

GLOBE Studies. (2006). Culture and Leadership. In P. G. Northouse (Ed.), *Leadership: Theory and Practice* (4th ed.). Sage.

House, R. J., Hanges, P. J., Javidan, M., Dorfman, P. W., & Gupta, V. (Eds.). (2004). *Culture, Leadership, and Organizations: The GLOBE Study of 62 Societies*. Sage Publications.

Hughes, M. (2018). Organizational Ambidexterity and Firm Performance: Burning Research Questions for Marketing Scholars. *Journal of Marketing Management, 34*(1–2), 178–229.

Hughes, M., Chang, Y. Y., Hodgkinson, I., Hughes, P., & Chang, C. Y. (2020). The Multi-Level Effects of Corporate Entrepreneurial Orientation on Business unit Radical Innovation and Financial Performance. *Long Range Planning, 54*(1), 101–989.

Hughes, M., & Weiss, J. (2007). Simple Rules for Making Alliances Work. *Harvard Business Review, 85*(11), 122–131.

Ireland, R. D., Hitt, M. A., & Sirmon, D. G. (2003). A Model of Strategic Entrepreneurship: The Construct and Its Dimensions. *Journal of Management, 29*(6), 963–989.

Jack, W., & Suri, T. (2011). *Mobile Money: The Economics of M-Pesa*. National Bureau of Economic Research.

Kompier, M. A., & Cooper, C. L. (1999). *Preventing Stress, Improving Productivity: European Case Studies in the Workplace*. Routledge.

Krause, D., & Pullman, M. (2021). Fighting to Survive: How Supply Chain Managers Navigate the Emerging Legal Cannabis Industry. *Journal of Supply Chain Management, 57*(3), 50–71.

Kuratko, D. F., & Audretsch, D. B. (2013). Clarifying the Domains of Corporate Entrepreneurship. *International Entrepreneurship and Management Journal, 9*(3), 323–335.

Lemley, M. A., & McCreary, A. (2021). Exit strategy. *BUL Review, 101*(1).

MacMillan, I. C., Siegel, R., & Narasimha, P. S. (1985). Criteria Used by Venture Capitalists to Evaluate New Venture Proposals. *Journal of Business Venturing, 1*(1), 119–128.

Mangaliso, M. P. (2001). Building Competitive Advantage from Ubuntu: Management Lessons from South Africa. *Academy of Management Executive, 15*(3), 22–33.

Mazzei, M. J., Ketchen, D. J., & Shook, C. L. (2017). Understanding Strategic Entrepreneurship: A 'Theoretical Toolbox' Approach. *International Entrepreneurship and Management Journal, 13*, 631–663.

McColl-Kennedy, J. R., & Anderson, R. D. (2002). Impact of Leadership Style and Emotions on Subordinate Performance. *The Leadership Quarterly, 13*(5), 545–559.

Northouse, P. G. (2007). *Leadership: Theory and Practice* (4th ed.). Sage.

Rauch, A., Wiklund, J., Lumpkin, G. T., & Frese, M. (2009). Entrepreneurial Orientation and Business Performance: An Assessment of Past Research and Suggestions for the Future. *Entrepreneurship Theory and Practice, 33*(3), 761–787.

Reid, S. W., Anglin, A. H., Baur, J. E., Short, J. C., & Buckley, M. R. (2018). Blazing New Trails or Opportunity Lost? Evaluating Research at the Intersection of Leadership and Entrepreneurship. *The Leadership Quarterly, 29*(1), 150–164.

Rosenbusch, N., Brinckmann, J., & Bausch, A. (2011). Is Innovation Always Beneficial? A Meta-Analysis of the Relationship Between Innovation and Performance in SMEs. *Journal of Business Venturing, 26*(4), 441–457.

Schoar, A. (2010). The Divide Between Subsistence and Transformational Entrepreneurship. In J. Lerner & S. Stern (Eds.), *Innovation Policy and the Economy* (Vol. 10, pp. 57–81). University of Chicago Press.

Simsek, Z. (2009). Organizational Ambidexterity: Towards a Multilevel Understanding. *Journal of Management Studies, 46*(4), 597–624.

Stinchcombe, A. L. (1965). Organizations and Social Structure. In *Handbook of Organizations* (Vol. 44, No. 2, pp. 142–193).

Tukker, A., & Tischner, U. (2017). *New Business for Old Europe: Product-Service Development*. Routledge.

Volery, T., Mueller, S., & von Siemens, B. (2015). Entrepreneur Ambidexterity: A Study of Entrepreneur Behaviours and Competencies in Growth-Oriented Small and Medium-Sized Enterprises. *International Small Business Journal, 33*(2), 109–129.

Voss, G. B., & Voss, Z. G. (2013). Strategic Ambidexterity in Small and Medium-Sized Enterprises: Implementing Exploration and Exploitation in Product and Market Domains. *Organization Science, 24*(5), 1459–1477.

Wanasika, I., Howell, J. P., Littrell, R., & Dorfman, P. (2011). Managerial Leadership and Culture in Sub-Saharan Africa. *Journal of World Business, 46*(2), 234–241.

Withers, M. C., Ireland, R. D., Miller, D., Harrison, J. S., & Boss, D. S. (2018). Competitive Landscape Shifts: The Influence of Strategic Entrepreneurship on Shifts in Market Commonality. *Academy of Management Review, 43*(3), 349–370.

Zach, S., & Baldegger, U. (2017). Leadership in Start-Ups. *International Small Business Journal, 35*, 157–177.

Zoogah, D. B. (2008). African Business Research: A Review of Studies Published in the Journal of African Business and a Framework for Enhancing Future Studies. *Journal of African Business, 9*(1), 219–255.

2

Historical and Institutional Contexts of Leadership in Africa

Leadership in Africa has deep historical roots, characterized by diverse and dynamic systems of governance that evolved over centuries.

2.1 Historical Foundations of Leadership in Africa

Pre-colonial Africa was marked by a variety of leadership structures, from centralized kingdoms to decentralized tribes and clans. Centralized kingdoms, such as the Ashanti Empire in present-day Ghana and the Zulu Kingdom in South Africa, had hierarchical systems with kings or chiefs wielding significant authority over political, economic, and military matters. These leaders were often viewed as semi-divine figures with spiritual and cultural significance, responsible for maintaining social order, defending the community, and ensuring the well-being of their people (Davidson, 1992). The Ashanti Empire, for instance, had a highly organized structure where the Asantehene (king) worked alongside a council of elders and various regional chiefs to govern effectively.

D. K. Amoo-Osae, Jr, *Self-Protective Leadership and Organizational Effectiveness*, Palgrave Studies in African Leadership, https://doi.org/10.1007/978-3-031-61308-1_2

In contrast, decentralized societies like the Igbo in Nigeria and the Kikuyu in Kenya operated through collective leadership. Decisions were made by councils of elders or community representatives, emphasizing consensus and collective responsibility. Leadership in these communities was more fluid and often rotated among different members based on merit and the ability to command respect and trust (Ong'ayo, 2008). The Igbo village assembly (Oha-na-Eze) and age-grade systems ensured that leadership was shared and distributed, promoting balance and fairness.

The advent of Islam and Christianity significantly influenced leadership in Africa. Islamic leaders, such as the Sultans and Emirs in West Africa, combined religious and political authority, promoting the spread of Islam and the establishment of Islamic institutions. Similarly, the introduction of Christianity brought about new forms of leadership, particularly through missionary schools and churches, which became important centers of influence and social change (Hastings, 1994). The Sokoto Caliphate in northern Nigeria, for example, was a powerful Islamic state that influenced political, economic, and religious life in the region.

Colonialism brought profound changes to African leadership. European powers imposed new administrative structures, often dismantling or co-opting existing traditional leadership systems. Colonial authorities appointed local chiefs based on loyalty to the colonial regime rather than legitimacy within their communities, leading to the erosion of traditional authority and creating divisions (Mamdani, 1996). The British policy of indirect rule in Nigeria, for instance, reshaped traditional chieftaincy roles, creating new power dynamics and altering indigenous governance systems.

Colonial education systems aimed to create a small elite class of Africans who could serve as intermediaries between the colonial administration and the local population. These elites were often educated in European languages and exposed to Western ideas, creating a distinct social class disconnected from traditional cultural roots. The colonial legacy of divide-and-rule policies further exacerbated ethnic and regional divisions, contributing to conflicts and power struggles in the post-independence era (Berman, 1998).

Despite these challenges, the colonial period also saw the emergence of nationalist movements and leaders who played pivotal roles in the struggle for independence. Leaders such as Kwame Nkrumah of Ghana, Jomo Kenyatta of Kenya, and Julius Nyerere of Tanzania emerged as influential figures advocating for self-determination and the end of colonial rule. These leaders drew on both traditional and modern leadership paradigms, blending indigenous values with nationalist ideologies (Meredith, 2005).

The post-independence period posed significant challenges for African leaders as they navigated the complexities of nation-building. Visionary leaders like Kwame Nkrumah, Jomo Kenyatta, and Nelson Mandela emerged as symbols of liberation and hope, but the transition from colonial rule to self-governance was fraught with difficulties. These leaders faced the daunting task of uniting ethnically diverse populations and addressing the legacies of colonialism, including economic underdevelopment and political fragmentation (Nugent, 2004).

Post-independence leaders faced immense pressure to deliver on promises of freedom and prosperity, often grappling with high expectations and limited resources. The transition from liberation movements to governing parties was complex, requiring strategic foresight and a commitment to inclusive governance (Nkomo & Hoobler, 2018). Many post-independence leaders centralized power, suppressed political opposition, and established one-party states, arguing that strong, centralized leadership was necessary for national unity and development. This approach often stifled political pluralism and led to human rights abuses (Bratton & van de Walle, 1997).

In response to the limitations of charismatic leadership, the 1980s and 1990s saw a shift toward more technocratic and managerial leadership styles. This period was characterized by the implementation of structural adjustment programs (SAPs) promoted by international financial institutions such as the World Bank and the International Monetary Fund (IMF). These programs emphasized economic liberalization, privatization, and public sector reform, leading to the rise of technocratic leaders who prioritized economic efficiency and governance reforms (Chabal & Daloz, 1999).

The end of the Cold War and the wave of democratization that swept across Africa in the late twentieth century further transformed leadership paradigms. Multi-party democracy, electoral competition, and civil society activism became more prominent, leading to the emergence of a new generation of leaders committed to democratic governance and political accountability. Leaders such as Nelson Mandela in South Africa and Ellen Johnson Sirleaf in Liberia symbolized this new era of leadership (Bratton & van de Walle, 1997). Despite these positive developments, post-independence leadership in Africa has also been marked by persistent challenges such as corruption, nepotism, and weak institutional capacity (Hyden, 2006).

2.2 Traditional Leadership Institutions

Traditional leadership institutions have played a crucial role in African societies for centuries. These institutions, rooted in the customs and traditions of various ethnic groups, have evolved over time and continue to influence contemporary leadership practices.

Traditional leadership institutions have historically been integral to African societies. Chiefs, kings, and elders served as mediators in disputes, custodians of land and resources, and keepers of cultural heritage. Their authority was deeply rooted in indigenous knowledge systems, oral histories, and customary laws, which guided community life and maintained social order (McCaskie, 1995; Ray & Reddy, 2003). These leaders were respected for their wisdom, experience, and moral authority, which were crucial for maintaining social cohesion and harmony within their communities.

In West Africa, for example, the Asantehene, the king of the Ashanti people in Ghana, holds a significant traditional leadership role. The Asantehene presides over the Ashanti Kingdom and plays a vital role in preserving Ashanti culture, customs, and heritage. The king's leadership is not just political but also spiritual, as he is considered the link between the living and the ancestors (McCaskie, 1995). The Golden Stool, the symbol of the Asantehene's power, embodies the unity and identity of the Ashanti people (Boahen, 1990).

Similarly, in Southern Africa, the Zulu King in South Africa holds a prominent traditional leadership position. The Zulu King is seen as the cultural and spiritual leader of the Zulu nation, responsible for upholding Zulu traditions and customs. The king's authority is deeply rooted in the historical legacy of the Zulu Kingdom and its founder, King Shaka Zulu (Hamilton, 1998). King Shaka's military innovations and statecraft laid the foundations for Zulu political structures that continue to influence the region.

Traditional leadership institutions also played significant roles in the administration of justice and the management of communal resources. In many societies, traditional leaders presided over customary courts, resolving disputes and ensuring that justice was served according to established customs and traditions. These leaders were also responsible for the equitable distribution of communal resources, such as land and water, ensuring that the needs of the community were met while maintaining sustainable practices (Ray & Reddy, 2003).

Over time, traditional leadership institutions have adapted to changing social, political, and economic contexts. The advent of colonialism brought significant disruptions to traditional leadership structures, as colonial powers sought to undermine indigenous authority and impose their own governance systems. However, many traditional leaders managed to maintain their roles and influence by integrating into new governance structures and adapting to colonial rule (Mamdani, 1996).

In some cases, colonial authorities co-opted traditional leaders, using them as intermediaries to implement colonial policies and maintain control over local populations. This strategy, known as indirect rule, allowed colonial administrations to govern vast territories with limited resources by relying on existing traditional hierarchies (Crowder, 1964). While this approach helped to preserve some aspects of traditional leadership, it also led to the manipulation and corruption of traditional leaders, who were often forced to prioritize colonial interests over the welfare of their communities.

The post-independence period brought further changes to traditional leadership institutions as newly independent African states sought to establish modern governance structures. In many countries, traditional leaders were incorporated into formal political systems, serving as advisors or representatives in local and national governments. This integration aimed to bridge the gap between traditional and modern governance systems, ensuring that the voices of local communities were heard in the policymaking process (Logan, 2009).

Today, traditional leadership remains relevant, especially in rural areas where formal state institutions may be weak or absent. Traditional leaders act as intermediaries between the government and local populations, facilitating communication and cooperation. They preside over customary courts, adjudicating disputes based on traditional laws and practices (Boege et al., 2009).

Traditional leaders are also involved in community development initiatives, leveraging their influence to mobilize resources and support for local projects. For example, traditional leaders in Ghana have been instrumental in promoting education and healthcare initiatives, working in partnership with government agencies and non-governmental organizations to improve the well-being of their communities (Ray & Reddy, 2003).

In some regions, traditional leadership has been instrumental in preserving cultural heritage and promoting tourism. For instance, in South Africa, the Zulu King plays a key role in cultural festivals and ceremonies that attract tourists and celebrate Zulu history and traditions. Similarly, in Nigeria, traditional leaders participate in festivals and cultural events that showcase the rich heritage of their communities, fostering a sense of pride and identity among the people (Afigbo, 1972).

Despite their resilience, traditional leadership institutions face numerous challenges in the modern era. The spread of formal education, urbanization, and the influence of Western legal and political systems have altered the dynamics of traditional leadership. Issues such as corruption, nepotism, and the manipulation of traditional leaders by political elites have undermined their credibility and effectiveness (van Kessel & Oomen, 1997).

Urbanization and modernization have led to a decline in the authority of traditional leaders, particularly among younger generations who are more influenced by contemporary values and lifestyles. The rise of formal education and employment opportunities in urban areas has also reduced the reliance on traditional leadership for guidance and support (Oomen, 2005).

However, traditional leadership institutions continue to adapt and evolve. In some countries, traditional leaders have been incorporated into formal political structures, serving as advisors or representatives in local and national governments. This integration aims to bridge the gap between traditional and modern governance systems, ensuring that the voices of local communities are heard in the policymaking process (Logan, 2009).

There are also opportunities to strengthen traditional leadership institutions through capacity-building initiatives and partnerships with development organizations. By enhancing the skills and knowledge of traditional leaders, these initiatives can help them address contemporary challenges more effectively and contribute to sustainable development in their communities. Programs that focus on leadership training, conflict resolution, and community development can empower traditional leaders to play a more active role in governance and development (Ray & Reddy, 2003).

2.3 Colonial Legacies and Leadership Development

The colonial era left an indelible mark on the leadership landscape in Africa. Colonial powers imposed Western governance models that disrupted existing traditional systems and significantly influenced the development of leadership on the continent.

Colonial administrations often appointed local chiefs and leaders based on their perceived loyalty to the colonial regime rather than their legitimacy within the community. This practice led to the creation of "warrant chiefs" in regions like Nigeria, where colonial authorities appointed individuals who did not necessarily have traditional claims to leadership. This disruption eroded the authority of legitimate traditional leaders and created divisions within communities (Mamdani, 1996).

Colonial powers imposed new administrative structures and governance models that prioritized their interests over the well-being of

African populations. These models often undermined traditional leadership systems, replacing them with centralized, bureaucratic structures that were easier to control. The imposition of Western legal and political systems further eroded the authority of traditional leaders and disrupted indigenous governance practices (Crowder, 1964).

Colonial education systems were designed to produce a small elite class of Africans who could serve as intermediaries between the colonial administration and the local population. These elites were often educated in European languages and exposed to Western ideas, creating a distinct social class disconnected from traditional cultural structures. The colonial legacy of divide-and-rule policies further exacerbated ethnic and regional divisions, contributing to conflicts and power struggles in the post-independence era (Berman, 1998).

Despite these challenges, the colonial period also saw the emergence of nationalist movements and leaders who played pivotal roles in the struggle for independence. Leaders such as Kwame Nkrumah, Jomo Kenyatta, and Julius Nyerere emerged as influential figures advocating for self-determination and the end of colonial rule. These leaders drew on both traditional and modern leadership paradigms, blending indigenous values with nationalist ideologies (Meredith, 2005).

Colonial legacies have also influenced the development of new leadership structures in post-independence Africa. The institutions and administrative frameworks established during the colonial period continued to shape governance practices, even after independence. This has resulted in a hybrid model of leadership that combines elements of traditional and Western governance systems. Many post-independence African states adopted centralized governance structures, modeled after their colonial predecessors, which often led to the concentration of power and the marginalization of traditional leadership institutions (Ake, 1993).

The enduring legacy of colonialism continues to influence leadership dynamics in post-colonial Africa, shaping patterns of governance, power relations, and socio-economic development. Many African countries grapple with the legacy of colonialism as the institutions and structures established during the colonial era continue to shape political and economic realities. Addressing the historical injustices and inequalities perpetuated by colonial rule remains a critical challenge for leadership development in Africa (Aina, 2010; Rotberg, 2014).

However, there are also opportunities to leverage the positive aspects of colonial legacies, such as the emphasis on formal education and administrative efficiency, to strengthen leadership development in Africa. By integrating traditional leadership values with modern governance practices, African countries can create more inclusive and effective leadership models that address the diverse needs of their populations. Programs that focus on capacity-building, leadership training, and the promotion of good governance can help to bridge the gap between traditional and modern leadership practices, fostering a more holistic approach to leadership development (Rotberg, 2014).

2.4 Post-independence Leadership Paradigms

The post-independence period in Africa marked a new era of leadership characterized by a mix of hope, challenges, and evolving paradigms. Newly independent African states faced the daunting task of nation-building, economic development, and political consolidation, all while navigating the complex legacies of colonialism.

One of the dominant leadership paradigms that emerged in the post-independence era was the model of charismatic leadership. Charismatic leaders such as Kwame Nkrumah, Jomo Kenyatta, and Julius Nyerere were seen as visionary figures who inspired their nations with promises of development, unity, and self-reliance. These leaders often drew on their personal charisma and revolutionary credentials to mobilize popular support and implement ambitious development agendas (Young, 1982). However, the concentration of power in the hands of charismatic leaders also led to challenges such as authoritarianism, political repression, and the erosion of democratic institutions.

Nkrumah's vision of Pan-Africanism and his efforts to unite African countries against colonial rule made him a seminal figure in Africa's independence movement. His leadership style, characterized by charisma and a strong centralizing approach, aimed to foster national unity and development but also faced criticism for authoritarian tendencies.

Kenyatta, a leader of the Mau Mau rebellion and later the first President of Kenya, embodied the fusion of traditional Kikuyu leadership with modern nationalist aspirations. His presidency focused on nation-building and economic development, although it also contended with ethnic divisions and political rivalries.

Nyerere's leadership in Tanzania was marked by his philosophy of Ujamaa (African socialism), which sought to blend traditional communal values with socialist principles. His emphasis on education, rural development, and national unity left a lasting impact on Tanzania's socio-political landscape.

In response to the limitations of charismatic leadership, the 1980s and 1990s saw a shift toward more technocratic and managerial leadership styles. This period was characterized by the implementation of structural adjustment programs (SAPs) promoted by international financial institutions such as the World Bank and the International Monetary Fund (IMF). These programs emphasized economic liberalization, privatization, and public sector reform, leading to the rise of technocratic leaders who prioritized economic efficiency and governance reforms (Chabal & Daloz, 1999).

During this time, many African countries experienced periods of authoritarian rule, where leaders consolidated power and suppressed political opposition in the name of stability and development. While authoritarianism may have initially promised stability and order, it often resulted in human rights abuses, corruption, and economic mismanagement. Leaders such as Mobutu Sese Seko in the Democratic Republic of Congo and Robert Mugabe in Zimbabwe exemplified the pitfalls of authoritarian rule, where personal power and control were prioritized over democratic governance and the well-being of the populace (Bayart, 1993).

The end of the Cold War and the wave of democratization that swept across Africa in the late twentieth century further transformed leadership paradigms. Multi-party democracy, electoral competition, and civil society activism became more prominent, leading to the emergence of a new generation of leaders committed to democratic governance and political accountability. Leaders such as Nelson Mandela in South Africa and Ellen Johnson Sirleaf in Liberia symbolized this new era of democratic leadership (Bratton & van de Walle, 1997).

Mandela's leadership in South Africa was instrumental in transitioning the country from apartheid to a democratic society. His emphasis on reconciliation, inclusivity, and human rights set a new standard for leadership on the continent. Similarly, Ellen Johnson Sirleaf, as Africa's first elected female head of state, brought significant reforms to Liberia, focusing on peacebuilding, economic recovery, and women's empowerment.

Despite these positive developments, the journey toward democratic governance in Africa has been fraught with challenges. Issues such as electoral fraud, political violence, and weak institutions have hindered the consolidation of democracy in many countries. Additionally, the persistence of corruption, nepotism, and weak institutional capacity continues to pose significant obstacles to democratic governance (Hyden, 2006).

Nonetheless, post-independence leadership in Africa has also been marked by persistent challenges such as corruption, nepotism, and weak institutional capacity. The struggle to balance traditional leadership values with modern governance demands continues to shape the leadership landscape in contemporary Africa (Hyden, 2006).

However, there are also numerous opportunities for enhancing leadership development on the continent. The increasing focus on good governance, transparency, and accountability provides a foundation for building stronger democratic institutions. Moreover, the growing role of civil society organizations, youth movements, and grassroots initiatives in advocating for democratic reforms and holding leaders accountable is a positive trend that can contribute to more inclusive and effective leadership (Branch & Cheeseman, 2009).

2.5 Institutional Approaches to Leadership Development

Institutional approaches to leadership development in Africa have evolved significantly over the years, reflecting the continent's changing socio-political and economic landscape. These approaches aim to equip leaders with the skills, knowledge, and values necessary to navigate the complex challenges of contemporary African societies.

One of the key institutional approaches to leadership development is the establishment of formal education and training programs. Universities, business schools, and leadership institutes across Africa offer a range of programs designed to develop the next generation of leaders. These programs often emphasize practical skills, ethical leadership, and strategic thinking, preparing leaders to address the specific challenges facing their countries and communities (Jackson, 2004).

For example, institutions such as the African Leadership University (ALU) and the African Management Institute (AMI) provide leadership training programs that combine academic rigor with real-world applications. These institutions focus on developing entrepreneurial and innovative leaders who can drive sustainable development and economic growth in Africa (Albright & Kuntze, 2013).

In addition to formal education, leadership development initiatives often include mentorship programs, networking opportunities, and experiential learning. Mentorship programs pair emerging leaders with experienced mentors who provide guidance, support, and insights based on their own leadership journeys. Networking opportunities, such as leadership forums and conferences, allow leaders to connect with peers, share experiences, and collaborate on solutions to common challenges (Day, 2001).

Experiential learning, such as leadership retreats, simulations, and community projects, provides leaders with hands-on experience in addressing real-world issues. These initiatives help leaders develop critical thinking, problem-solving, and decision-making skills, as well as foster a sense of social responsibility and community engagement (Kolb, 1984).

Despite the advancements in institutional approaches to leadership development, several challenges remain. One of the primary challenges is the accessibility and inclusivity of these programs. Many leadership development initiatives are concentrated in urban areas and may not be accessible to potential leaders in rural or marginalized communities. Additionally, the cost of participating in leadership programs can be prohibitive for many individuals, limiting the reach and impact of these initiatives (Aina, 2010).

Another challenge is the alignment of leadership development programs with the specific needs and contexts of African societies. Many leadership curricula are based on Western models and may not fully address the unique challenges and opportunities present in African contexts. There is a need for leadership development programs that are culturally relevant and tailored to the socio-economic and political realities of the continent (Bolden & Kirk, 2009).

There are several opportunities to enhance leadership development in Africa. One such opportunity is the integration of indigenous knowledge and practices into leadership training programs. By incorporating traditional leadership values and practices, leadership development initiatives can become more relevant and effective in addressing the needs of African communities. This approach can also help to bridge the gap between traditional and modern leadership systems, fostering a more holistic understanding of leadership (Ambe-Uva, 2010).

Furthermore, leveraging technology and digital platforms can expand the reach of leadership development programs. Online courses, webinars, and virtual mentorship programs can provide accessible and flexible learning opportunities for aspiring leaders across the continent. This approach can also facilitate knowledge-sharing and collaboration among leaders from different regions and sectors, promoting a more interconnected and resilient leadership network (OECD, 2021).

Regional and international partnerships play a significant role in enhancing leadership development in Africa. Collaborations between African institutions and international organizations, universities, and development agencies facilitate the exchange of knowledge, resources, and best practices. These partnerships help to build the capacity of African leadership institutions and support the development of a robust leadership ecosystem (Thomas, 2008).

References

Afigbo, A. E. (1972). *The Warrant Chiefs: Indirect Rule in Southeastern Nigeria, 1891–1929*. Cambridge University Press.

Aina, T. A. (2010). Beyond Reforms: The Politics of Higher Education Transformation in Africa. *African Studies Review, 53*(1), 21–40.

Ake, C. (1993). What Is the Problem of Ethnicity in Africa? *Transformation, 22*, 1–14.

Albright, M. D., & Kuntze, R. (2013). Virtual Team Trust: The Role of Leadership and Technology. *Business Management Dynamics, 3*(2), 13–21.

Ambe-Uva, T. N. (2010). Open and Distance Education in Nigeria: The Administrative Challenges. *The Turkish Online Journal of Distance Education, 11*(2), 58–69.

Bayart, J.-F. (1993). *The State in Africa: The Politics of the Belly*. Longman.

Berman, B. J. (1998). *Ethnicity, Patronage and the African State: The Politics of Uncivil Nationalism*. Lynne Rienner Publishers.

Boahen, A. A. (1990). *Africa Under Colonial Domination 1880–1935*. James Currey Publishers.

Branch, D., & Cheeseman, N. (2009). Democratization, Sequencing, and state Failure in Africa: Lessons from Kenya. *African Affairs, 108*(430), 1–26.

Bratton, M., & van de Walle, N. (1997). *Democratic Experiments in Africa: Regime Transitions in Comparative Perspective*. Cambridge University Press.

Boege, V., Brown, A., & Clements, K. P. (2009). Hybrid Political Orders, Not Fragile States. *Peace Review: A Journal of Social Justice, 21*(1), 13–21.

Bolden, R., & Kirk, P. (2009). African Leadership Surfacing New Understandings Through Leadership Development. *International Journal of Cross Cultural Management, 9*(1), 69–86.

Chabal, P., & Daloz, J. P. (1999). *Africa Works: Disorder as Political Instrument*. Indiana University Press.

Crowder, M. (1964). Indirect Rule: French and British Style. *Africa: Journal of the International African Institute, 34*(3), 197–205.

Davidson, B. (1992). *The Black Man's Burden: Africa and the Curse of the Nation-State*. James Currey Publishers.

Day, D. V. (2001). Leadership Development: A Review in Context. *The Leadership Quarterly, 11*(4), 581–613.

Hamilton, C. (1998). *Terrific Majesty: The Powers of Shaka Zulu and the Limits of Historical Invention*. Harvard University Press.

Hastings, A. (1994). *The Church in Africa 1450–1950*. Clarendon Press.

Hyden, G. (2006). *African Politics in Comparative Perspective*. Cambridge University Press.

Jackson, T. (2004). *Management and Change in Africa: A Cross-cultural Perspective*. Routledge.

Kolb, D. A. (1984). *Experiential Learning: Experience as the Source of Learning and Development*. Prentice Hall.

Logan, C. (2009). Selected Chiefs, Elected Councillors, and Hybrid Democrats: Popular Perspectives on the Co-existence of Democracy and Traditional Authority. *The Journal of Modern African Studies, 47*(1), 101–128.

Mamdani, M. (1996). *Citizen and Subject: Contemporary Africa and the Legacy of Late Colonialism*. Princeton University Press.

McCaskie, T. C. (1995). *State and Society in Pre-colonial Asante*. Cambridge University Press.

Meredith, M. (2005). *The State of Africa: A History of Fifty Years of Independence*. Free Press.

Nkomo, S., & Hoobler, J. M. (2018). A Historical Perspective on African Leadership: Setting the Stage for the Next Generation. In S. Nkomo & J. M. Hoobler (Eds.), *African Leadership: Perspectives on Leadership in Africa* (pp. 1–20). Emerald Publishing Limited.

Nugent, P. (2004). *Africa Since Independence: A Comparative History*. Palgrave Macmillan.

Oomen, B. (2005). *Chiefs in South Africa: Law, Power & Culture in the Post-Apartheid Era*. University of KwaZulu-Natal Press.

Ong'ayo, A. O. (2008). *Political Instability in Africa: Where the Problem Lies and Alternative Perspectives*. The African Diaspora Policy Centre.

Organisation for Economic Co-operation and Development. (2021). *OECD Economic Outlook 2021*. OECD Publishing.

Ray, D. I., & Reddy, P. S. (2003). *Grassroots Governance? Chiefs in Africa and the Afro-Caribbean*. University of Calgary Press.

Rotberg, R. I. (2014). *Africa Emerges: Consummate Challenges, Abundant Opportunities*. Polity Press.

van Kessel, I., & Oomen, B. (1997). One Chief, One Vote: The Revival of Traditional Authorities in Post-Apartheid South Africa. *African Affairs, 96*(385), 561–585.

Young, C. (1982). The African Colonial State in Comparative Perspective. *Comparative Politics, 14*(2), 127–146.

3

Self-Protective Leadership: Scope and Essence

3.1 Definition and Significance

What Is Self-Protective Leadership

Self-Protective Leadership (SPL) is a contemporary leadership approach that emphasizes the leader's well-being and self-care as essential components of their effectiveness and influence within an organization. Traditionally, leadership models have focused on external factors such as influencing and motivating others. However, SPL shifts this focus to include the leader's self-care and personal development, recognizing that leaders who maintain their well-being are better equipped to lead others, manage stress, and make sound decisions (Goleman, 1998).

At its core, SPL encompasses a range of practices and behaviors aimed at protecting the leader's physical, emotional, and mental health. These practices include managing stress, setting boundaries, practicing emotional intelligence, and fostering resilience. By prioritizing these aspects, leaders can maintain high levels of performance and sustain their leadership effectiveness over the long term (Kompier & Cooper, 1999). This holistic approach not only benefits the leaders themselves but also

D. K. Amoo-Osae, Jr, *Self-Protective Leadership and Organizational Effectiveness*, Palgrave Studies in African Leadership, https://doi.org/10.1007/978-3-031-61308-1_3

positively impacts their teams and organizations, creating a healthier and more productive work environment.

Why SPL Matters: Its Impact and Importance

The significance of SPL is particularly pronounced in high-stress environments such as start-ups, where leaders often face intense pressures and challenges. Start-up leaders are typically responsible for driving the vision and strategy of the organization while also managing daily operations, securing funding, and navigating market competition. This dual role can lead to significant stress and burnout if not managed effectively (Nielsen & Munir, 2009).

SPL provides a framework that helps leaders manage these challenges by integrating self-care into their leadership approach. This not only enhances their personal well-being but also positively impacts their ability to lead and inspire their teams. Leaders who practice SPL are more resilient, emotionally intelligent, and better equipped to handle the complexities of their roles (Goleman et al., 2002). They can navigate the unpredictable nature of start-ups with a calm and focused mindset, setting the stage for long-term success.

Moreover, SPL has broader implications for organizational culture and performance. Leaders who prioritize their well-being set a positive example for their teams, fostering a culture of health and productivity. This can lead to higher employee engagement, reduced turnover, and improved organizational outcomes. In this way, SPL contributes to both the personal development of leaders and the overall success of the organization (Avolio & Gardner, 2005). By creating a supportive and balanced work environment, leaders can attract and retain top talent, driving innovation and growth.

3.2 Aspects of Self-Protective Leadership

SPL is a multifaceted approach that encompasses several key aspects, each contributing to the overall effectiveness and well-being of the leader. These aspects are personal well-being, emotional intelligence, resilience and adaptability, work-life integration, authenticity, boundary setting, proactive stress management, and continuous learning. Each dimension plays a crucial role in shaping a well-rounded and effective leader.

Personal Well-Being

Personal well-being is a foundational aspect of SPL. It encompasses the physical, emotional, and mental health of the leader. Leaders who maintain their personal well-being are better equipped to handle stress, make sound decisions, and sustain their leadership effectiveness over time (Kabat-Zinn, 1990).

Maintaining physical health involves regular exercise, a balanced diet, adequate sleep, and regular medical check-ups. Physical well-being is crucial for sustaining energy levels and preventing burnout. Leaders who prioritize their physical health are more likely to have the stamina and resilience needed to navigate the demands of their roles (Kompier & Cooper, 1999). For instance, leaders who engage in regular physical activity report higher levels of energy and productivity, allowing them to tackle challenges head-on.

Emotional health involves managing stress, maintaining a positive outlook, and seeking support when needed. Leaders who are emotionally healthy are better equipped to handle the pressures of their roles and maintain a positive and productive work environment. Practices such as mindfulness, meditation, and seeking therapy can contribute to emotional well-being (Goleman, 1998). Emotionally healthy leaders are better able to foster a supportive and collaborative team culture, leading to higher levels of employee satisfaction and performance.

Mental health is about maintaining cognitive function and mental clarity. This includes practices such as continuous learning, intellectual engagement, and mental relaxation techniques. Leaders who prioritize their mental health are better able to think strategically, solve problems, and innovate (Senge, 1990). For example, leaders who engage in regular intellectual pursuits, such as reading or attending workshops, are better equipped to generate innovative solutions and drive organizational growth.

Emotional Intelligence

Emotional intelligence (EI) is the ability to recognize, understand, and manage one's own emotions and the emotions of others. It is a critical component of SPL as it directly impacts a leader's ability to connect with their team, manage stress, and make informed decisions (Goleman, 1998).

Self-awareness is the foundation of emotional intelligence. It involves understanding one's own emotions, strengths, weaknesses, and values. Leaders who are self-aware can better manage their reactions to stress and challenges, and make decisions that align with their core values (Goleman, 1995). Self-aware leaders can also identify their own triggers and develop strategies to manage them effectively, leading to more consistent and thoughtful decision-making.

Self-regulation involves managing one's emotions and impulses. Leaders who can self-regulate are able to stay calm under pressure, maintain focus, and respond to challenges in a measured and thoughtful manner. This ability is crucial for maintaining a stable and productive work environment (Goleman, 1998). For instance, leaders who practice self-regulation are less likely to react impulsively to stressful situations, allowing them to maintain a calm and composed demeanor.

Motivation refers to the inner drive to achieve goals and succeed. Leaders with high motivation are passionate about their work, set high standards for themselves and their teams, and are committed to achieving their vision. This inner drive is a key component of SPL as it sustains leaders through challenges and setbacks (Ryan & Deci, 2000). Motivated leaders are better able to inspire and energize their teams, creating a culture of high performance and achievement.

Empathy is the ability to understand and share the feelings of others. Leaders who practice empathy are able to build strong relationships with their teams, foster a supportive work environment, and address the needs and concerns of their employees. Empathy is crucial for creating a culture of trust and collaboration (Goleman, 1998). Empathetic leaders can better understand their team members' perspectives and provide the support and guidance needed to help them succeed.

Social skills involve the ability to build and maintain relationships, communicate effectively, and manage conflicts. Leaders with strong social skills are able to create cohesive teams, navigate organizational dynamics, and foster a positive and productive work environment (Goleman, 1998).

Resilience and Adaptability

Resilience and adaptability are essential components of SPL, particularly in the fast-paced and often uncertain environment of start-ups. Resilience refers to the ability to recover from setbacks and challenges, while adaptability involves being flexible and open to change (Coutu, 2002).

Building resilience involves developing coping strategies for stress, maintaining a positive outlook, and seeking support when needed. Leaders who are resilient are better able to handle the ups and downs of their roles and sustain their effectiveness over the long term (Kompier & Cooper, 1999). Fostering adaptability involves being open to new ideas, willing to change course when necessary, and staying flexible in the face of uncertainty. Leaders who are adaptable can navigate the rapidly changing environment of start-ups and seize new opportunities as they arise (Heifetz et al., 2009).

Learning from failure is a critical aspect of resilience and adaptability. Leaders who view failure as an opportunity for growth and learning are better able to bounce back from setbacks and continue to drive their organizations forward (Dweck, 2006).

Work-Life Integration

Work-life integration is about finding a balance between work responsibilities and personal life. For start-up leaders, this balance can be particularly challenging given the demands of their roles. However, achieving work-life integration is crucial for maintaining long-term well-being and effectiveness (Greenhaus & Beutell, 1985).

Setting boundaries involves establishing clear limits between work and personal life. This can include setting specific work hours, creating a dedicated workspace, and taking regular breaks. By setting boundaries, leaders can ensure they have time to recharge and maintain their well-being (Ashforth et al., 2000). Prioritizing self-care involves making time for activities that promote physical, emotional, and mental well-being. This can include exercise, hobbies, spending time with loved ones, and relaxation. Leaders who prioritize self-care are better equipped to handle the demands of their roles and sustain their effectiveness over time (Kabat-Zinn, 1990).

Flexible work arrangements, such as remote work or flexible hours, can help leaders achieve work-life integration. These arrangements allow leaders to balance their work responsibilities with personal commitments and reduce stress (Hill et al., 1996).

Authenticity

Authenticity involves being true to oneself and acting in alignment with one's values and beliefs. Authentic leaders are transparent, honest, and trustworthy, which helps to build a strong and positive organizational culture (Avolio & Gardner, 2005).

Being true to oneself involves understanding one's values, strengths, and weaknesses, and acting in a way that is consistent with these. Authentic leaders are self-aware and genuine, which helps to build trust and credibility with their teams (Kernis, 2003). Building trust involves being transparent, honest, and reliable. Authentic leaders are open about their intentions and actions, which helps to create a culture of trust and collaboration within the organization (Meyer et al., 1995). Leading with integrity involves acting in accordance with one's values and principles. Authentic leaders make decisions that align with their values, even when it is difficult or unpopular. This consistency helps to build a strong and positive organizational culture (Ciulla, 2004).

Boundary Setting

Boundary setting is about establishing clear limits and guidelines for oneself and others. This can help leaders manage their workload, reduce stress, and maintain a healthy work-life balance (Ashforth et al., 2000).

Establishing clear guidelines involves setting expectations for oneself and others. This can include setting limits on work hours, defining roles and responsibilities, and creating clear communication channels. By setting clear guidelines, leaders can ensure that their time and energy are used effectively (Kreiner et al., 2009). Managing workload involves prioritizing tasks, delegating responsibilities, and saying no to non-essential activities. Leaders who manage their workload effectively are better able to focus on high-priority tasks and maintain their well-being (Cox, 2003). Creating a supportive environment involves fostering a culture of respect and collaboration. Leaders who set clear boundaries and encourage others to do the same create a positive and productive work environment (Kossek & Lambert, 2005).

Proactive Stress Management

Proactive stress management involves taking steps to prevent and manage stress before it becomes overwhelming. This can help leaders maintain their well-being and sustain their effectiveness over the long term (Lazarus & Folkman, 1984).

Identifying stressors involves recognizing the factors that contribute to stress. This can include work demands, personal commitments, and environmental factors. By identifying stressors, leaders can take steps to manage them effectively (Kabat-Zinn, 1990). Developing coping strategies involves finding ways to manage stress and maintain well-being.

This can include mindfulness practices, exercise, and relaxation techniques. Leaders who develop effective coping strategies are better able to handle the demands of their roles (Cox, 2003). Seeking support involves reaching out to others for help and advice. This can include talking to colleagues, seeking professional counseling, or joining support groups. Leaders who seek support are better able to manage stress and maintain their well-being (House, 1981).

Continuous Learning

Continuous learning involves staying abreast of industry trends, technological advancements, and market dynamics. Leaders who embrace continuous learning foster a culture of innovation and adaptability within their organizations (Senge, 1990).

Staying informed involves keeping up to date with the latest developments in one's field. This can include reading industry publications, attending conferences, and participating in professional development programs. Leaders who stay informed are better able to make informed decisions and drive their organizations forward (Drucker, 1985). Encouraging innovation involves creating an environment that supports creativity and experimentation. This can include fostering a culture of continuous improvement, encouraging risk-taking, and providing resources for innovation. Leaders who encourage innovation are better able to drive growth and success (Amabile, 1996). Fostering a learning culture involves promoting continuous learning and development within the organization. This can include providing training opportunities, encouraging knowledge sharing, and supporting professional development. Leaders who foster a learning culture create a dynamic and adaptable organization (Garvin, 1993).

3.3 Navigating Africa's Unique Business Challenges

The African business landscape is a multifaceted terrain shaped by a confluence of historical, cultural, and institutional factors that influence the conduct of business and leadership practices across the continent (Acemoglu & Robinson, 2006). With 54 countries encompassing diverse socio-economic contexts and cultural backgrounds, Africa presents both opportunities and challenges for businesses and leaders alike.

Africa's vast natural resources, including minerals, arable land, and renewable energy sources, underscore its potential for economic growth and development (Ndlela & Mpofu, 2015). However, the exploitation of these resources has been fraught with challenges, including political instability, weak governance structures, and corruption, which have hindered sustainable development efforts (Mauro, 1995).

Political instability and governance deficits remain pervasive in many African countries, leading to regulatory complexities, policy uncertainties, and increased risk for businesses (Bratton & van de Walle, 1997). Moreover, corruption, both in the public and private sectors, poses significant obstacles to business operations, stifling investment, hindering competition, and eroding public trust (Kaufmann, 1997).

Socio-economic disparities further complicate the African business landscape, with stark contrasts between countries with robust infrastructural development and vibrant business ecosystems and those facing entrenched poverty, inadequate access to basic services, and underdeveloped markets (Ndlela & Mpofu, 2015). These disparities create uneven opportunities for businesses and exacerbate socio-economic inequalities within and between countries.

Cultural diversity is another hallmark of the African business landscape, with each country boasting its own set of cultural norms, values, and business practices (Hofstede, 2001). While cultural diversity enriches the business environment and fosters innovation, it also presents challenges in terms of cross-cultural communication, negotiation, and relationship-building.

Africa's integration into the global economy brings both opportunities and challenges for businesses, with globalization opening up new markets, facilitating trade and investment, and fostering technological innovation. However, it also exposes African businesses to increased competition, market volatility, and external shocks, necessitating adaptive strategies and resilience in the face of global uncertainties.

3.4 Case Scenarios of SPL in the African Sociopolitical Context

The prevalence of self-protective leadership in the African business landscape stems from a combination of factors, including historical legacies, cultural norms, and institutional weaknesses. Historical experiences of colonization, resource exploitation, and political instability have shaped perceptions of leadership and power dynamics in many African societies (Nkurunziza & Bates, 2018). Additionally, cultural values such as collectivism, respect for authority, and loyalty to kinship networks often influence leadership behaviors, sometimes reinforcing self-protective tendencies (Aycan et al., 2000).

Empirical research and case studies provide valuable insights into the manifestations and consequences of self-protective leadership in African businesses. For example, a study by Okoye and Ezejiofor (2019) examined self-protective leadership behaviors among Nigerian business leaders, highlighting how a lack of accountability and weak governance structures contribute to the prevalence of such behaviors. Similarly, research by Chitakunye and Kang'ethe (2018) explored the impact of self-protective leadership on employee morale and organizational performance in Zimbabwe, demonstrating the negative effects of leader-centered decision-making and favoritism.

Furthermore, case studies from various African countries offer compelling examples of self-protective leadership in action. In South Africa, for instance, the political and business landscape has been marred by allegations of corruption and cronyism, with leaders prioritizing personal gain over the interests of the broader society (Ndletyana, 2019). Similarly, in Angola, leaders have been accused of using their positions of power to enrich themselves and their inner circles, often at the expense of public resources and economic development (Gumede, 2020; Matondo, 2016; Mutongwizo & Mutongwizo, 2020).

In Ghana, a notable example of self-protective leadership can be seen in the case of the National Youth Employment Programme (NYEP). Despite its noble intentions to address youth unemployment, the program was plagued by reports of mismanagement, embezzlement of funds, and political favoritism (Amoako-Gyampah & Acquaah, 2008). Leaders within the program were accused of prioritizing personal interests and political allegiances over the effective implementation of the program, ultimately undermining its impact on job creation and economic development.

Similarly, in Kenya, self-protective leadership has been observed in various sectors, including politics and business. The Goldenberg scandal, one of the largest financial scandals in Kenyan history, involved senior government officials and business leaders colluding to defraud the government of billions of shillings through illegal gold exports (Barkan, 2009). This case exemplifies how self-protective behaviors among leaders can lead to widespread corruption, erode public trust, and impede socio-economic progress.

In Nigeria, the fuel subsidy scandal is a prominent example of self-protective leadership. This scandal involved senior government officials and oil marketers colluding to defraud the government through inflated claims for fuel subsidy payments. Investigations revealed that billions of dollars were siphoned off through fraudulent subsidy claims, leading to significant financial losses for the Nigerian government and taxpayers (Barkindo & Salihu, 2018). This scandal exposed the pervasive corruption and self-serving practices among political and business elites in Nigeria.

In Tanzania, the Richmond scandal revolved around a dubious contract awarded to Richmond Development Company to supply emergency electricity-generating units. The contract was characterized by irregularities, including lack of transparency and inflated costs, leading to suspicions of corruption and kickbacks involving high-ranking government officials (Kweka, 2014). The Richmond scandal underscored the challenges of corruption and lack of accountability in Tanzania's governance systems.

The maizegate scandal in Zambia involved allegations of corruption and irregularities in the procurement of maize for the country's Food Reserve Agency (FRA). It was revealed that government officials had authorized the importation of maize at inflated prices from private suppliers, leading to significant financial losses for the government and taxpayers (Mwale, 2018). The maizegate scandal exposed the vulnerabilities in Zambia's public procurement processes and raised concerns about accountability and transparency in government operations.

In Zimbabwe, the Grain Marketing Board (GMB) Grain Scandal involved allegations of corruption and mismanagement within the state-owned grain procurement agency. It was discovered that senior officials at the GMB had inflated maize purchase prices and engaged in fraudulent activities, resulting in significant financial losses for the government and undermining food security efforts in the country (Ndlovu, 2020). The scandal exposed the systemic corruption and lack of accountability within Zimbabwe's public institutions.

In the Democratic Republic of Congo (DRC), numerous scandals related to the mining sector have arisen. Leaders have been accused of granting lucrative mining contracts to foreign companies in exchange for personal enrichment. These contracts often lack transparency and accountability, leading to allegations of corruption and exploitation of natural resources at the expense of the Congolese people (Raftopoulos, 2018). The mining contracts scandal reflects the challenges of governance and resource management in the DRC.

In Uganda, the Temangalo Land Scandal involved allegations of corruption and fraudulent land deals between government officials and private developers. It was revealed that prime government land in Temangalo had been sold at below-market prices to a private developer with close ties to high-ranking officials (Kiggundu, 2011). The scandal exposed the collusion between political leaders and business interests, highlighting the challenges of corruption and lack of accountability in Uganda's governance systems.

Operation Sparrowhawk in Cameroon was a government-led anti-corruption campaign aimed at tackling corruption and embezzlement within state institutions. However, the campaign was criticized for its selective prosecution of political opponents and perceived lack of transparency (Kamdem, 2013). Critics argued that Operation Sparrowhawk was used as a tool to consolidate power and suppress dissent rather than genuinely combatting corruption and promoting accountability.

The Hidden Debt Scandal in Mozambique involved the secret borrowing of billions of dollars by the government to finance maritime projects without parliamentary approval or public disclosure. The loans were arranged by state-owned companies and foreign banks, with the involvement of senior government officials (Blanthorne, 2017). The scandal led to a debt crisis, economic downturn, and suspension of international aid, highlighting the consequences of self-serving leadership and lack of transparency in Mozambique's governance.

In Ethiopia, the construction of the Grand Ethiopian Renaissance Dam (GERD) has been marred by allegations of corruption and mismanagement. Reports of inflated costs, irregular procurement practices, and lack of transparency in project financing have raised concerns about the involvement of political elites and business interests in the dam project (Tadesse, 2020). The GERD project highlights the challenges of governance and accountability in Ethiopia's development initiatives.

During the reign of former President Omar al-Bashir, Sudan experienced widespread corruption and mismanagement across various sectors, including government, business, and natural resource extraction. The regime was accused of embezzling public funds, manipulating contracts for personal gain, and suppressing dissent through authoritarian measures (Ibrahim, 2019). The corruption under the Al Bashir regime contributed to economic stagnation and widespread public discontent, culminating in mass protests and eventually the ousting of the president in 2019.

In Somalia, corruption in the distribution of humanitarian aid has been a persistent issue, particularly during times of conflict and humanitarian crisis. Aid intended for vulnerable populations, including food, medicine, and shelter, has often been diverted by corrupt officials and local leaders for personal enrichment or political gain (Menkhaus, 2010). The misappropriation of aid resources has exacerbated humanitarian suffering and hindered efforts to address poverty and insecurity in Somalia.

Corruption and mismanagement in the cocoa sector have been long-standing issues in Ivory Coast, one of the world's largest producers of cocoa beans. Government officials and industry stakeholders have been implicated in various corrupt practices, including smuggling, tax evasion, and exploitation of child labor (Lahsen & Salgado, 2020). The corruption in the cocoa sector has perpetuated poverty among cocoa farmers, undermined regulatory efforts, and tarnished the country's reputation as a leading cocoa exporter.

In Malawi, the Cashgate Scandal involved the systematic looting of public funds through fraudulent government contracts, inflated procurement prices, and ghost workers on the government payroll. The scandal, which came to light in 2013, revealed the extent of corruption and financial mismanagement within the government, leading to public outrage and calls for accountability (Kasambala, 2017). The Cashgate scandal underscored the challenges of governance and transparency in Malawi's public institutions.

The Firestone rubber plantation in Liberia has faced allegations of labor exploitation and human rights abuses, including child labor, unsafe working conditions, and low wages. Despite being one of the largest employers in the country, Firestone has been criticized for its failure to uphold labor standards and protect the rights of workers (Smith, 2018). The exploitation of labor at the Firestone plantation reflects broader issues of corporate accountability and governance in Liberia's business sector.

These empirical findings and case studies underscore the pervasive nature of self-protective leadership in the African business landscape and its detrimental impact on organizational effectiveness, employee well-being, and societal development. By shedding light on the root causes and consequences of self-protective behaviors among leaders, researchers and practitioners can develop targeted interventions and strategies aimed at promoting ethical and effective leadership practices in African businesses and organizations.

3.5 Bringing It All Together: The Value of SPL

In the exploration of self-protective leadership, we have traversed a transformative landscape that redefines the traditional contours of leadership. Rooted in the recognition that a leader's well-being is intrinsically linked to their ability to guide and inspire others, self-protective leadership emerges as a holistic and forward-thinking paradigm encompassing dimensions that span personal well-being, emotional intelligence, resilience, adaptability, authenticity, boundary setting, proactive stress management, and continuous learning.

At its essence, self-protective leadership signifies a departure from conventional leadership models, acknowledging that leadership effectiveness transcends the influence a leader has on their team to include the leader's personal journey of growth, self-awareness, and well-being. The commitment to personal well-being, a cornerstone of self-protective leadership, emphasizes that leaders functioning at their best are those who intentionally nurture their physical, mental, and emotional health.

Embracing emotional intelligence as a critical dimension, self-protective leaders not only navigate intricate interpersonal dynamics but also foster a workplace culture that values empathy, communication, and collaboration. The emphasis on resilience and adaptability positions leaders not only as adept navigators of change but also as catalysts for a culture of continuous learning and innovation within their teams.

The scope of self-protective leadership expands further into work-life integration, challenging the traditional notion of work-life balance by acknowledging the interconnectedness of personal and professional life. Leaders who model such integration contribute not only to their own satisfaction and well-being but also foster an organizational culture that values a harmonious blend of personal and professional pursuits.

The dimensions of authenticity and boundary setting underscore the importance of leaders aligning their actions with their values while establishing clear limits to prevent burnout. By cultivating authenticity, leaders create an environment where team members feel empowered to be their true selves, fostering trust and collaboration. Proactive stress management further solidifies this foundation, emphasizing the need for leaders to address stressors effectively and contribute to a workplace culture that values mental health.

Continuous learning, the final dimension, encapsulates the commitment to ongoing development, industry awareness, and a culture of curiosity and innovation. Leaders who prioritize continuous learning not only stay abreast of industry changes but also embody the adaptability and openness required to thrive in the dynamic organizational landscape.

In conclusion, self-protective leadership is a comprehensive and adaptive response to the evolving challenges faced by leaders in contemporary organizations. By prioritizing personal well-being, embracing emotional intelligence, fostering resilience, and continuously learning, leaders can navigate the intricacies of leadership with authenticity and effectiveness. Self-protective leadership is not just a model; it is a call to reshape our understanding of leadership as a dynamic and reciprocal relationship between the leader and their team, where both parties flourish in an environment that values well-being, growth, and collaboration. As organizations strive for success in an ever-changing world, self-protective leadership emerges as a beacon guiding leaders toward a more sustainable and impactful leadership journey.

References

Acemoglu, D., & Robinson, J. A. (2006). *Economic Origins of Dictatorship and Democracy*. Cambridge University Press.

Amabile, T. M. (1996). *Creativity in Context: Update to the Social Psychology of Creativity*. Westview Press.

Amoako-Gyampah, K., & Acquaah, M. (2008). Leadership Effectiveness, Leadership Style and Employee Readiness. *Leadership & Organization Development Journal, 29*(5), 450–464.

Ashforth, B. E., Kreiner, G. E., & Fugate, M. (2000). All in a Day's Work: Boundaries and Micro Role Transitions. *Academy of Management Review, 25*(3), 472–491.

Avolio, B. J., & Gardner, W. L. (2005). Authentic Leadership Development: Getting to the Root of Positive Forms of Leadership. *The Leadership Quarterly, 16*(3), 315–338.

Aycan, Z., Kanungo, R. N., Mendonca, M., Yu, K., Deller, J., Stahl, G., & Khursid, A. (2000). Impact of Culture on Human Resource Management Practices: A 10-Country Comparison. *Applied Psychology, 49*(1), 192–221.

Barkan, J. D. (2009). *Kenya: A History Since Independence*. Indiana University Press.

Barkindo, M. S., & Salihu, A. (2018). Fuel Subsidy Removal and The Nigerian Economy: A Policy Option. *International Journal of Energy Economics and Policy, 8*(4), 183–191.

Blanthorne, A. (2017). Mozambique: The Hidden Debt Scandal. *African Affairs, 116*(462), 190–200.

Bratton, M., & van de Walle, N. (1997). *Democratic Experiments in Africa: Regime Transitions in Comparative Perspective*. Cambridge University Press.

Chitakunye, P., & Kang'ethe, S. M. (2018). The Influence of Self-Protective Leadership on Morale and Organizational Performance in the Zimbabwean Civil Service. *Journal of Public Affairs, 18*(4), e1732.

Ciulla, J. B. (2004). *Ethics, the Heart of Leadership* (2nd ed.). Praeger.

Coutu, D. L. (2002). How Resilience Works. *Harvard Business Review, 80*(5), 46–55.

Cox, T. (2003). *Stress Research and Stress Management: Putting Theory to Work*. HSE Books.

Drucker, P. F. (1985). *Innovation and Entrepreneurship: Practice and Principles*. Harper & Row.

Dweck, C. S. (2006). *Mindset: The New Psychology of Success*. Random House.

Garvin, D. A. (1993). Building a Learning Organization. *Harvard Business Review, 71*(4), 78–91.

Goleman, D. (1995). *Emotional Intelligence: Why It Can Matter More Than IQ*. Bantam Books.

Goleman, D. (1998). What Makes a Leader? *Harvard Business Review, 76*(6), 93–102.

Goleman, D., Boyatzis, R., & McKee, A. (2002). *Primal Leadership: Realizing the Power of Emotional Intelligence*. Harvard Business School Press.

Greenhaus, J. H., & Beutell, N. J. (1985). Sources of Conflict Between Work and Family Roles. *Academy of Management Review, 10*(1), 76–88.

Gumede, W. M. (2020). *Africa: State of Crisis: What Went Wrong and What Can Be Done About It*. Wits University Press.

Heifetz, R. A., Grashow, A., & Linsky, M. (2009). *The Practice of Adaptive Leadership: Tools and Tactics for Changing Your Organization and the World*. Harvard Business Press.

Hill, E. J., Hawkins, A. J., & Miller, B. C. (1996). Work and Family in the Virtual Office: Perceived Influences of Mobile Telework. *Family Relations, 45*(3), 293–301.

Hofstede, G. (2001). *Culture's Consequences: Comparing Values, Behaviors, Institutions, and Organizations Across Nations*. Sage.

House, R. J. (1981). A Path Goal Theory of Leader Effectiveness. *Administrative Science Quarterly, 16*(3), 321–339.

Ibrahim, A. S. (2019). The impact of leadership styles on employee performance in Nigerian universities. Journal of Management Development, 38(2), 112–125.

Kabat-Zinn, J. (1990). *Full Catastrophe Living: Using the Wisdom of Your Body and Mind to Face Stress, Pain, and Illness*. Delacorte Press.

Kamdem, P. (2013). The Pitfalls of Anti-Corruption Campaigns in Cameroon: The Case of Operation Sparrowhawk. *African Journal of Political Science and International Relations, 7*(2), 76–84.

Kasambala, T. (2017). Corruption and Governance in Malawi: The Cashgate Scandal. *Journal of Developing Societies, 33*(3), 337–354.

Kaufmann, D. (1997). Corruption: The Facts. *Foreign Policy, 107*, 114–131.

Kernis, M. H. (2003). Toward a Conceptualization of Optimal Self-Esteem. *Psychological Inquiry, 14*(1), 1–26.

Kiggundu, M. N. (2011). *Uganda: The Challenge of Growth And Poverty Reduction*. World Bank Publications.

Kompier, M. A., & Cooper, C. L. (1999). *Preventing Stress, Improving Productivity: European Case Studies in the Workplace*. Routledge.

Kossek, E. E., & Lambert, S. J. (Eds.). (2005). *Work and Life Integration: Organizational, Cultural, and Individual Perspectives*. Lawrence Erlbaum Associates.

Kreiner, G. E., Hollensbe, E. C., & Sheep, M. L. (2009). Balancing Borders and Bridges: Negotiating the Work-Home Interface via Boundary Work Tactics. *Academy of Management Journal, 52*(4), 704–730.

Kweka, A. (2014). *Tanzania: An African 'Success Story' in Crisis*. Zed Books.

Lahsen, A., & Salgado, A. M. (2020). Corruption in the Ivorian Cocoa Sector: Assessing the Impact on Smallholder Cocoa Farmers. *Journal of Business Ethics, 163*(2), 299–317.

Lazarus, R. S., & Folkman, S. (1984). *Stress, Appraisal, and Coping*. Springer.

Matondo, C. (2016). "Angola's Elusive Development Path: Prospects and Challenges." In *The Palgrave Handbook of African Politics, Governance and Development* (pp. 421–434). Palgrave Macmillan.

Mauro, P. (1995). Corruption and Growth. *The Quarterly Journal of Economics, 110*(3), 681–712.

Menkhaus, K. (2010). Governance Without Government in Somalia: Spoilers, State Building, and the Politics of Coping. *International Security, 31*(3), 74–106.

Meyer, J. P., Davis, S. L., & Schoorman, F. D. (1995). An Integrative Model of Organizational Trust. *Academy of Management Review, 20*(3), 709–734.

Mutongwizo, T., & Mutongwizo, P. (2020). Political Corruption and Its Impact on Economic Development in Angola. In *Corruption and Development in Africa* (pp. 239–253). Palgrave Macmillan.

Mwale, T. (2018). Zambia Maizegate: A Case of Food Security at the Mercy of Corruption. *Journal of Public Administration and Governance, 8*(1), 309–322.

Ndlela, L. L., & Mpofu, T. M. (2015). *Economic Transformation in Africa.* Springer.

Ndletyana, M. (2019). *Political Corruption in South Africa: Before, During and After State Capture.* In *Handbook of Political Party Funding* (pp. 309–324). Edward Elgar Publishing.

Ndlovu, N. (2020). The Grain Scandal: Corruption and Mismanagement in Zimbabwe's Grain Marketing Board. *Journal of African Studies and Development, 12*(4), 61–75.

Nielsen, K., & Munir, F. (2009). How Do Transformational Leaders Influence Followers' Affective Well-Being? Exploring the Mediating Role of Self-Efficacy. *Work & Stress, 23*(4), 313–329.

Nkurunziza, J. D., & Bates, R. H. (2018). Colonial Legacies, Political Identities, and Leadership in Africa. *Comparative Political Studies, 51*(3), 275–306.

Okoye, A., & Ezejiofor, R. (2019). Self-Protective Leadership Behaviors and Organizational Performance: Evidence from Nigerian Business Leaders. *Journal of Leadership Studies, 13*(2), 122–134.

Raftopoulos, B. (2018). Mining and Political Conflict in the Democratic Republic of Congo. In *Mining in Africa* (pp. 209–224). Palgrave Macmillan.

Ryan, R. M., & Deci, E. L. (2000). Self-Determination Theory and the Facilitation of Intrinsic Motivation, Social Development, and Well-Being. *American Psychologist, 55*(1), 68–78.

Senge, P. M. (1990). *The Fifth Discipline: The Art and Practice of the Learning Organization.* Doubleday.

Smith, J. (2018). Labor Exploitation and Human Rights Abuses in the Firestone Rubber Plantation in Liberia. *Journal of Business Ethics, 47*(2), 221–236.

Tadesse, F. (2020). Grand Ethiopian Renaissance Dam: A Critical Analysis of Ethiopia's Largest Infrastructure Project. *African Journal of Science, Technology, Innovation and Development, 12*(4), 441–457.

Walumbwa, F. O., Avolio, B. J., & Gardner, W. L. (2005). Authentic Leadership: Development and Validation of a Theory-Based Measure. *Journal of Management, 34*(1), 89–126.

Walumbwa, F. O., Avolio, B. J., Gardner, W. L., Wernsing, T. S., & Peterson, S. J. (2008). Psychological Processes Linking Authentic Leadership to Follower Behaviors. *Leadership Quarterly, 19*(6), 765–783.

4

Models of Organizational Leadership Behavior

4.1 Leadership Concepts and Themes

Leadership involves guiding and influencing others to achieve common goals, characterized by various concepts and themes that provide insight into the dynamics of leadership in organizational settings.

Influence and Power: Leadership fundamentally involves the exercise of influence and power. Leaders use their position, authority, and personal attributes to shape the attitudes, behaviors, and actions of their followers. This influence can be formal, derived from a leader's official position within an organization, or informal, stemming from personal charisma, expertise, or relationships (Yukl, 2013). For instance, Steve Jobs' ability to influence his team at Apple was not just because of his role as CEO but also due to his visionary ideas and persuasive communication skills (French & Raven, 1959).

Motivation and Inspiration: Effective leadership involves motivating and inspiring followers to achieve organizational goals. This includes creating a vision that excites and engages people, as well as fostering a sense of purpose and commitment. Motivational leadership taps into the intrinsic and extrinsic needs of followers, driving them toward higher performance levels (Ryan & Deci, 2000). For example, Nelson Mandela's

D. K. Amoo-Osae, Jr, *Self-Protective Leadership and Organizational Effectiveness*, Palgrave Studies in African Leadership, https://doi.org/10.1007/978-3-031-61308-1_4

leadership during the apartheid era in South Africa inspired millions to strive for equality and justice, demonstrating how a compelling vision can drive collective action (Bass, 1985).

Change and Innovation: Leaders play a critical role in driving change and fostering innovation within organizations. They identify opportunities for improvement, challenge the status quo, and encourage creative thinking. Leadership in this context involves managing the dynamics of change, overcoming resistance, and guiding organizations through transitions (Lewin, 1951). Jeff Bezos, founder of Amazon, exemplifies this by continuously pushing for innovation, from revolutionizing online shopping to advancing cloud computing services (Kotter, 1996).

Communication and Vision: Clear and effective communication is essential for successful leadership. Leaders must be able to articulate their vision and goals in a way that resonates with their followers. This involves not only the transmission of information but also active listening and engaging in meaningful dialogue (Covey, 1989). Oprah Winfrey's success can be attributed to her exceptional communication skills and ability to connect with her audience on a deep, emotional level (Hackman & Johnson, 2013).

Emotional Intelligence: The ability to understand and manage one's own emotions and those of others is a crucial leadership skill. Leaders with high emotional intelligence are better equipped to handle interpersonal relationships judiciously and empathetically, which enhances their ability to lead effectively (Mayer & Salovey, 1997). For instance, Satya Nadella, CEO of Microsoft, has been praised for his empathetic leadership style, which has helped transform the company's culture and foster greater innovation and collaboration (Goleman, 1995).

4.2 Leadership Styles and Their Impact

Different leadership styles have distinct impacts on organizational behavior and performance. Understanding these styles helps leaders to adapt their approach based on the needs of their team and the organizational context.

Autocratic Leadership: Autocratic leaders make decisions unilaterally without seeking input from others. This style can be effective in situations requiring quick decision-making and strong direction. However, it can also lead to low morale and disengagement among team members, as they may feel undervalued and disempowered (Blake & Mouton, 1964). A historical example is Henry Ford, whose autocratic style helped streamline production in the early days of Ford Motor Company but also led to high employee turnover and dissatisfaction (Lewin et al., 1939).

Democratic Leadership: Democratic leaders involve their followers in decision-making processes. This style fosters a sense of ownership and accountability among team members, leading to higher levels of engagement and satisfaction. However, it can be time-consuming and may not be suitable for situations requiring rapid decisions (Hackman & Johnson, 2013). An example is Google's leadership approach, where input from employees is highly valued and often integrated into the decision-making process, fostering a culture of innovation and collaboration (Bass & Avolio, 1994).

Laissez-Faire Leadership: Laissez-faire leaders provide minimal guidance and allow their followers to make their own decisions. This style can be effective when team members are highly skilled and self-motivated, as it fosters creativity and innovation. However, it can also lead to a lack of direction and coordination, resulting in inefficiency and poor performance (Yukl, 2013). An example is Warren Buffett's leadership style at Berkshire Hathaway, where he provides broad strategic direction but allows managers of subsidiary companies significant autonomy (Bass, 1990).

Transformational Leadership: Transformational leaders inspire and motivate their followers to achieve higher levels of performance and personal development. They create a compelling vision, communicate it effectively, and foster an environment of trust and collaboration. This style is particularly effective for driving change and innovation within the organization (Burns, 1978). An example is Elon Musk, whose transformational leadership at SpaceX and Tesla has driven significant advancements in space exploration and electric vehicles (Bass, 1985).

Transactional Leadership: Transactional leaders use a system of rewards and punishments to achieve compliance and performance. This style is effective for maintaining order and achieving short-term goals but may not be sufficient for fostering long-term growth and development. It can lead to a transactional mindset among team members, where they are motivated primarily by external rewards rather than intrinsic motivation (Bass & Riggio, 2006). An example is Jack Welch's tenure at General Electric, where his transactional approach focused on performance metrics and financial results (Burns, 1978).

Servant Leadership: Servant leaders prioritize the needs and well-being of their followers, fostering a supportive and empowering work environment. This style is effective for building strong relationships and creating a positive organizational culture. It also promotes employee engagement and well-being, which are critical for long-term success (Spears, 1995). An example is Howard Schultz, former CEO of Starbucks, who focused on employee satisfaction and community engagement, leading to a strong corporate culture and brand loyalty (Greenleaf, 1977).

Charismatic Leadership: Charismatic leaders possess a magnetic personality and the ability to inspire and influence others through their vision and communication skills. This style can be highly effective in rallying support and driving organizational change. However, it also carries the risk of creating dependency on the leader and can be less effective in situations that require collective decision-making and collaboration (Conger & Kanungo, 1998). An example is Richard Branson, whose charismatic leadership has helped build the Virgin Group into a global brand (Weber, 1947).

4.3 Theoretical Perspectives on Leadership

Theoretical perspectives on leadership provide a deeper understanding of the principles and mechanisms that underpin effective leadership behavior. These theories offer insights into the various factors that influence leadership effectiveness and guide the development of leadership strategies.

Behavioral Leadership Theory: Behavioral theory focuses on the actions and behaviors of leaders rather than their inherent traits. This theory suggests that effective leadership is based on learned behaviors and actions, such as task-oriented and relationship-oriented behaviors. Behavioral theory emphasizes that leadership can be developed through training and practice. For example, successful leaders often develop their skills through experience and feedback, continually refining their approach to better meet the needs of their organization (Blake & Mouton, 1964). Moreover, Northouse (2019) highlights that behavioral theory provides a practical framework for leadership development by identifying specific actions that leaders can adopt to enhance their effectiveness.

Contingency Leadership Theory: Contingency theory posits that the effectiveness of leadership is contingent upon the situation and context in which it is applied. Different situations require different leadership styles and approaches. Contingency theory emphasizes the importance of adaptability and flexibility in leadership. For instance, a leader in a high-stress, crisis situation may adopt a more directive style, while in a stable environment, a more participative approach might be effective (Fiedler, 1967). Similarly, House (1971) argues that contingency theory allows leaders to match their behaviors to the specific demands of their organizational environment, thereby improving overall performance.

Relational Leadership Theory: Relational leadership theory focuses on the importance of relationships between leaders and followers. It emphasizes the role of social interactions and mutual influence in shaping leadership dynamics. This theory posits that effective leadership is rooted in the quality of relationships and the ability to foster trust, respect, and collaboration. For example, leaders who build strong, positive relationships with their team members are more likely to achieve high levels of performance and satisfaction (Uhl-Bien, 2006). Additionally, Graen and Uhl-Bien (1995) suggest that relational leadership theory underscores the significance of leader-member exchange (LMX) in enhancing employee engagement and productivity.

Complexity Leadership Theory: Complexity leadership theory addresses the dynamic and adaptive nature of leadership in complex organizational environments. It emphasizes the interplay between formal and informal leadership processes, highlighting the importance of emergent leadership behaviors that arise in response to complex and unpredictable challenges. This theory advocates for adaptive, flexible, and distributed leadership approaches. For instance, in fast-paced industries like technology, leaders must navigate constant change and innovation, requiring a more fluid and collaborative leadership style (Uhl-Bien et al., 2007). Marion and Uhl-Bien (2001) add that complexity leadership fosters innovation by enabling networks of individuals to self-organize and respond dynamically to emerging challenges.

Implicit Leadership Theory: Implicit leadership theory explores the cognitive processes underlying leadership perceptions and behaviors. It suggests that individuals have implicit assumptions and mental models about what constitutes effective leadership, which influence their evaluations of leaders and leadership behaviors. Understanding these implicit beliefs can help leaders align their behaviors with followers' expectations. For example, leaders who are aware of their team's expectations can tailor their approach to better meet these implicit standards, enhancing their effectiveness (Eden & Leviatan, 1975). Epitropaki and Martin (2004) argue that implicit leadership theory also helps uncover biases in leader evaluations, enabling more objective assessments of leadership effectiveness.

Situational Leadership Theory: Situational leadership theory posits that leaders should adapt their styles based on the maturity level of their followers. This theory emphasizes the importance of versatile, adaptive actions in different situations to achieve desired outcomes (Hersey & Blanchard, 1977). For instance, leaders may adopt a directive approach when followers require close supervision or a supportive style when followers are more experienced and confident (Hersey & Blanchard, 1977). Yukl (2013) reinforces that situational leadership provides a flexible framework for leaders to adjust their behaviors to meet the evolving needs of their teams effectively.

4.4 The Self-Protective Leadership Paradigm

The self-protective leadership paradigm prioritizes ensuring the safety and security of the individual or group through status enhancement and face-saving. This style involves being self-centered, status-conscious, a conflict inducer, focused on face-saving, and procedural. It is more acceptable in some cultures than in others and can influence an individual's likelihood of becoming an entrepreneur (House et al., 2004). Research shows that self-protective leadership is often associated with collectivist cultures where maintaining harmony and upholding status are key (Dorfman et al., 2012).

Self-Centered: Self-centered leaders aim to control the entire organization, often following an idiosyncratic decision-making style and using their administrative influence to engage in self-destructive behavior. Such leaders may prioritize their own interests over organizational goals, which can hinder growth and sustainability. For example, over-centralization of power by self-centered leaders often stifles innovation and discourages employee participation (Northouse, 2019).

Self-Conscious: Self-consciousness is crucial in leadership, encompassing both positive and negative emotions. It relates to how the leader's self-awareness and perception of their role influence organizational outcomes. Self-conscious leaders may exhibit heightened sensitivity to criticism, which can either enhance their resilience or lead to over-cautiousness in decision-making. Research indicates that self-conscious leadership can positively impact the survival of start-up businesses when coupled with strategic adaptability (Ashkanasy & Daus, 2005).

Conflict Inducer: Conflict-inducing leaders can cause interpersonal tension within organizations. While traditionally viewed as detrimental, conflict can sometimes serve as a catalyst for growth, fostering innovation and encouraging interdependence among team members. Rahim (2011) highlights that managed conflict can lead to better decision-making and problem-solving, while unmanaged conflict induced by such leaders may erode trust and collaboration.

Face-Saving: Face-saving is essential for communication and relationship-building in leadership. Leaders must relate to others, find commonalities, and work toward shared goals. In collectivist cultures, face-saving practices are especially significant, as they preserve harmony and prevent public embarrassment. Ting-Toomey (2005) notes that effective face-saving leadership can enhance cross-cultural negotiations and stakeholder relationships.

Procedural: Procedural leaders emphasize following established protocols and formalities to maintain order and control. By ensuring that processes are systematic and methodical, procedural leadership prioritizes stability and predictability within organizations. While this approach can enhance efficiency, it may also hinder flexibility and creativity in dynamic environments (Mintzberg, 1980). Procedural leadership works best in industries where standardization and consistency are critical, such as manufacturing or healthcare.

4.5 Strategic Entrepreneurial Behavior

Strategic entrepreneurship behavior (SEB) is a leadership approach that combines strategic thinking with entrepreneurial action. It involves the ability to identify and exploit opportunities, innovate, and drive organizational growth while aligning actions with long-term strategic goals (Ireland et al., 2003). This concept is crucial for businesses aiming to sustain growth and adapt in rapidly changing environments (Hitt et al., 2011).

Opportunity Recognition: Opportunity recognition is the ability to identify emerging opportunities in the market and develop innovative solutions to capitalize on them. This involves staying attuned to industry trends, technological advancements, and market dynamics. Successful entrepreneurs excel at recognizing gaps in the market and leveraging their insights to create value. For instance, Elon Musk's ventures into electric vehicles with Tesla and space exploration with SpaceX exemplify this ability to recognize and act on new opportunities. Musk saw the potential for sustainable energy and advanced space travel long before they became mainstream, positioning his companies as leaders in these fields (Vance, 2017). In the African context, M-Pesa in Kenya identified a significant gap in financial services, particularly among the unbanked population. The platform allowed users to perform financial transactions using their mobile phones, revolutionizing the financial sector in Kenya and beyond (Hughes & Lonie, 2007).

Resource Mobilization: Effective resource mobilization involves securing funding, building strategic partnerships, and attracting top talent. This is critical for scaling operations and achieving sustainable growth. Entrepreneurs need to be adept at identifying and leveraging various resources to support their ventures. For instance, Airbnb's founders leveraged their network to secure early investments and partnerships, which were crucial for the company's growth. They transformed their idea of renting air mattresses into a global hospitality platform by effectively utilizing the resources at their disposal (Gallagher, 2017). In Ghana, Zipline, a drone delivery service, has demonstrated effective resource mobilization by partnering with the Ghanaian government to deliver medical supplies to remote areas. Their collaboration with global investors has provided the necessary funding to scale their innovative solution (Kamenetz, 2019).

Culture of Innovation: Creating a culture of innovation is pivotal for strategic entrepreneurship. This involves fostering an environment that encourages experimentation, risk-taking, and continuous learning. Organizations that cultivate a culture of innovation are better positioned to adapt to changes and drive growth. Google's 20%-time policy, which allows employees to spend part of their time on innovative projects, has led to the development of successful products like Gmail and Google Maps (Schmidt & Rosenberg, 2014). In Nigeria, Flutterwave, a fintech company, has created a culture of innovation by continuously developing new solutions to facilitate online payments. Their commitment to innovation has positioned them as a leading payment platform in Africa, enabling businesses to accept payments in various forms and currencies (Ogunjobi, 2021).

Decision-Making Skills: Strategic entrepreneurs need strong decision-making skills to navigate uncertainty and manage risk. Effective decision-making involves analyzing data, assessing potential outcomes, and weighing the pros and cons of different options. This skill is crucial for seizing opportunities and overcoming challenges. For example, Netflix's decision to pivot from DVD rentals to streaming services involved significant risk but ultimately led to the company's success.

This strategic move required comprehensive market analysis, foresight, and a willingness to embrace change (Hastings & Meyer, 2020). In South Africa, Naspers, a global consumer internet group, demonstrated strategic decision-making by investing early in technology companies like Tencent. This decision has paid off immensely, transforming Naspers into one of the most significant tech investors globally (Clark, 2017).

Strategic entrepreneurship behavior combines visionary thinking with pragmatic execution, driving sustainable growth and innovation. Entrepreneurs in Africa, such as those at M-Pesa, Zipline, Flutterwave, and Naspers, exemplify how strategic opportunity recognition, resource mobilization, fostering a culture of innovation, and decisive action can lead to remarkable success.

4.6 Dynamics of Starting a Business

Entrepreneurship is crucial for economic growth, and many countries strive to create an "enterprise culture" to support business creation and expansion. Start-ups face challenges such as the liability of newness and smallness, but strategic leadership and entrepreneurial behavior can help overcome these obstacles and drive success (Stinchcombe, 1965).

Liability of Newness and Smallness: New ventures often face higher risks of failure due to limited resources and inexperience. This phenomenon, known as the liability of newness and smallness, makes it challenging for start-ups to compete with established firms. Overcoming these challenges requires strategic leadership and innovative thinking. The founders of Warby Parker addressed the liability of newness by creating a strong brand identity and offering a unique value proposition of affordable, stylish eyewear. They mitigated risks by utilizing a direct-to-consumer model, which reduced costs and built a loyal customer base (Blake, 2016). In Ghana, the start-up Farmerline is tackling the liability of newness by providing digital tools and information to farmers to increase their productivity and market access. By leveraging technology, Farmerline offers a unique value proposition that addresses the specific needs of smallholder farmers, helping them overcome the challenges associated with starting a new agricultural venture (Bempah, 2018).

Support Systems and Networks: Access to networks and support systems, including mentorship, incubators, and industry associations, is vital for start-ups. These resources provide essential guidance, resources, and opportunities for collaboration. Y Combinator, a renowned start-up accelerator, has helped launch successful companies like Dropbox and Airbnb by providing start-ups with seed funding, mentorship, and access to a network of investors and industry experts. This support has significantly increased their chances of success (Lacy, 2011). In Kenya, the iHub has become a pivotal support system for tech entrepreneurs, providing a collaborative space for innovation, networking opportunities, and access to funding. The iHub has supported numerous start-ups in scaling their operations and achieving success, demonstrating the critical role that support systems play in the entrepreneurial ecosystem (Bosire, 2016).

Regulatory and Market Conditions: Navigating regulatory environments and market conditions is critical for start-up success. Understanding local regulations, market dynamics, and competitive landscapes allows entrepreneurs to make informed decisions and develop effective strategies. Grab, a Southeast Asian ride-hailing company, successfully navigated the complex regulatory landscape by working closely with local governments and adapting their business model to meet local needs. This strategic approach enabled Grab to expand rapidly and become a dominant player in the region (Hill, 2019). In Nigeria, Andela, a company that trains software developers and connects them with global tech companies, has successfully navigated the regulatory and market conditions by working closely with government officials and understanding the local talent landscape. Andela's strategic approach has enabled it to tap into Nigeria's vast pool of tech talent, creating significant opportunities for both developers and the tech industry (Helm, 2019).

Sustainable Growth: Achieving sustainable growth involves balancing short-term achievements with long-term objectives. Entrepreneurs must focus on building scalable business models, maintaining financial health, and fostering a culture of continuous improvement and innovation. Patagonia's commitment to sustainability and ethical business practices has driven long-term success by investing in environmental initiatives and maintaining transparency in its supply chain. This approach has fostered customer loyalty and sustained growth (Chouinard, 2016). In South Africa, Woolworths has demonstrated a commitment to sustainable growth through its Good Business Journey, focusing on reducing environmental impact, promoting ethical sourcing, and improving social outcomes. This comprehensive approach to sustainability has helped Woolworths build a strong brand reputation and achieve long-term success in the retail sector (Woolworths Holdings Limited, 2020).

Expanding on the dynamics of starting a business with real-world examples and case scenarios provides practical insights for entrepreneurs. The stories of Farmerline, iHub, Andela, and Woolworths highlight the importance of strategic leadership, resourcefulness, and adaptability in navigating the challenges of entrepreneurship. These examples illustrate how effective strategies and innovative thinking can drive start-up success and long-term growth in the African context.

References

Ashkanasy, N. M., & Daus, C. S. (2005). Rumors of the Death of Emotional Intelligence in Organizational Behaviour are Vastly Exaggerated. *Journal of Organizational Behavior, 26*(4), 441–452.

Bass, B. M. (1985). *Leadership and Performance Beyond Expectations*. Free Press.

Bass, B. M. (1990). *Bass & Stogdill's Handbook of Leadership: Theory, Research, and Managerial Applications* (3rd ed.). Free Press.

Bass, B. M., & Avolio, B. J. (1994). *Improving Organizational Effectiveness Through Transformational Leadership*. Sage Publications.

Bass, B. M., & Riggio, R. E. (2006). *Transformational Leadership*. Psychology Press.

Bempah, K. (2018). *Farmerline: Bridging the Gap for African Farmers Through Technology*. GhanaWeb.

Blake, P. (2016). *The Visionaries Behind Warby Parker*. Forbes.

Blake, R. R., & Mouton, J. S. (1964). *The managerial grid: Key orientations for achieving production through people*. Gulf Publishing Company.

Bosire, M. (2016). *How iHub Is Transforming Kenya's Tech Ecosystem*. TechCabal.

Burns, J. M. (1978). *Leadership*. Harper & Row.

Chouinard, Y. (2016). *Let My People Go Surfing: The Education of a Reluctant Businessman*. Penguin Books.
Clark, D. (2017). *Alibaba: The House That Jack Ma Built*. Harper Business.
Conger, J. A., & Kanungo, R. N. (1998). *Charismatic Leadership in Organizations*. Sage Publications.
Covey, S. R. (1989). *The 7 Habits of Highly Effective People*. Simon & Schuster.
Dorfman, P. W., Javidan, M., Hanges, P. J., Dastmalchian, A., & House, R. J. (2012). GLOBE: A Twenty-Year Journey into the Intriguing World of Culture and Leadership. *Journal of World Business, 47*(4), 504–518.
Eden, D., & Leviatan, U. (1975). Implicit Leadership Theory as a Determinant of the Factor Structure Underlying Supervisory Behavior Scales. *Journal of Applied Psychology, 60*(6), 736–741.
Fiedler, F. E. (1967). *A Theory of Leadership Effectiveness*. McGraw-Hill.
French, J. R. P., & Raven, B. (1959). The Bases of Social Power. In D. Cartwright (Ed.), *Studies in Social Power* (pp. 150–167). University of Michigan.
Gallagher, L. (2017). *The Airbnb Story: How Three Ordinary Guys Disrupted an Industry, Made Billions of Dollars ... and Created Plenty of Controversy*. Mariner Books.
Goleman, D. (1995). *Emotional intelligence: Why iI Can Matter More Than IQ*. Bantam Books.
Goleman, D. (2000). Leadership That Gets Results. *Harvard Business Review, 78*(2), 78–90.
Graen, G. B., & Uhl-Bien, M. (1995). Relationship-Based Approach to Leadership: Development of Leader-Member Exchange (LMX) Theory of Leadership Over 25 Years. *Leadership Quarterly, 6*(2), 219–247.
Greenleaf, R. K. (1977). *Servant Leadership: A Journey into the Nature of Legitimate Power and Greatness*. Paulist Press.
Hackman, J. R., & Johnson, C. E. (2013). *Leadership: A Communication Perspective* (6th ed.). Waveland Press.
Hastings, R., & Meyer, E. (2020). *No Rules Rules: Netflix and the Culture of Reinvention*. Penguin Press.
Helm, S. (2019). *Andela: Bridging the Global Tech Talent Gap*. Harvard Business Review.
Hersey, P., & Blanchard, K. H. (1977). *Management of Organizational Behavior: Utilizing Human Resources*. Prentice-Hall.
Hill, S. (2019). *The Grab Story: Navigating Southeast Asia's Ride-Hailing Landscape*. MIT Sloan Review.

Hitt, M. A., Ireland, R. D., Sirmon, D. G., & Trahms, C. A. (2011). Strategic Entrepreneurship: Creating Value for Individuals, Organizations, and Society. *Academy of Management Perspectives, 25*(2), 57–75.

House, R. J., Hanges, P. J., Javidan, M., Dorfman, P., & Gupta, V. (2004). *Culture, Leadership, and Organizations: The GLOBE Study of 62 Societies.* Sage Publications.

House, R. J. (1971). An Overview of the GLOBE Research Program. In R. J. House, P. J. Hanges, M. Javidan, P. W. Dorfman, & V. Gupta (Eds.), *Culture, Leadership, and Organizations: The GLOBE Study of 62 Societies* (pp. 29–53). Sage Publications.

Hughes, N., & Lonie, S. (2007). M-Pesa: Mobile Money for the "Unbanked." *Innovations, 2*(1–2), 63–81.

Ireland, R. D., Hitt, M. A., & Sirmon, D. G. (2003). A Model of Strategic Entrepreneurship: The Construct and Its Dimensions. *Journal of Management, 29*(6), 963–989.

Kamenetz, A. (2019). *Zipline's Medical Delivery Drones in Ghana.* National Public Radio (NPR).

Kotter, J. P. (1996). *Leading Change.* Harvard Business Review Press.

Lacy, S. (2011). *Brilliant, Crazy, Cocky: How the Top 1% of Entrepreneurs Profit from Global Chaos.* John Wiley & Sons.

Lewin, K. (1951). *Field Theory in Social Science.* Harper & Row.

Lewin, K., Lippitt, R., & White, R. K. (1939). Patterns of Aggressive Behavior in Experimentally Created Social Climates. *The Journal of Social Psychology, 10*(2), 271–299.

Marion, R., & Uhl-Bien, M. (2001). Leadership in Complex Organizations. *Leadership Quarterly, 12*(4), 389–418.

Mayer, J. D., & Salovey, P. (1997). What Is Emotional Intelligence? In P. Salovey & D. Sluyter (Eds.), *Emotional Development and Emotional Intelligence: Educational Implications* (pp. 3–31). Basic Books.

Mintzberg, H. (1980). Structure in 5's: A Synthesis of the Research on Organization Design. *Management Science, 26*(3), 322–341.

Northouse, P. G. (2019). *Leadership: Theory and Practice* (8th ed.). Sage Publications.

Ogunjobi, R. (2021). *Flutterwave: The Fintech Redefining Online Payments in Africa.* TechCabal.

Rahim, M. A. (2011). *Managing Conflict in Organizations.* Transaction Publishers.

Ryan, R. M., & Deci, E. L. (2000). Self-determination Theory and the Facilitation of Intrinsic Motivation, Social Development, and Well-being. *American Psychologist, 55*(1), 68–78.

Schmidt, E., & Rosenberg, J. (2014). *How Google Works*. Grand Central Publishing.

Spears, L. C. (1995). *Reflections on Leadership: How Robert K. Greenleaf's Theory of Servant Leadership Influenced Today's Top Management Thinkers*. Wiley.

Stinchcombe, A. L. (1965). *Social Structure and Organizations*. Handbook of Organizations.

Ting-Toomey, S. (2005). The Matrix of Face: An Updated Face-negotiation Theory. In W. B. Gudykunst (Ed.), *Theorizing About Intercultural Communication* (pp. 71–92). Sage Publications.

Uhl-Bien, M. (2006). Relational Leadership Theory: Exploring the Social Processes of Leadership and Organizing. *Leadership Quarterly, 17*(6), 654–676.

Uhl-Bien, M., Marion, R., & McKelvey, B. (2007). Complexity Leadership Theory: Shifting Leadership from the Industrial Age to the Knowledge Era. *Leadership Quarterly, 18*(4), 298–318.

Vance, A. (2017). *Elon Musk: Tesla, SpaceX, and the Quest for a Fantastic Future*. Harper Business.

Weber, M. (1947). *The Theory of Social and Economic Organization* [(A. M. Henderson & T. Parsons, Trans.) Original Work Published 1922]. Oxford University Press.

Woolworths Holdings Limited. (2020). *The Good Business Journey: 2020 Sustainability Report*. Woolworths South Africa.

Yukl, G. (2013). *Leadership in Organizations* (8th ed.). Pearson.

5

From Theory to Empirics: Self-Protective Leadership and Organizational Effectiveness

This chapter examines the interplay between the attributes of Self-Protective Leadership (SPL) and start-up businesses survival. SPL attributes include self-centeredness, status-consciousness, conflict induction, face-saving, and procedural adherence. The survival of start-up businesses is the dependent variable, with strategic entrepreneurial behavior acting as a moderating variable. This framework aims to understand how each SPL attribute affects a leader's performance and the business's longevity (House et al., 2004).

5.1 Conceptual Model and Hypotheses

A. **Self-Centered Dimension of SPL**

Self-centered leaders prioritize their own needs over others, often isolating themselves. According to the GLOBE study, self-centeredness negatively impacts global leadership effectiveness (House et al., 2004). Thus, the hypothesis is:

D. K. Amoo-Osae, Jr, *Self-Protective Leadership and Organizational Effectiveness*, Palgrave Studies in African Leadership, https://doi.org/10.1007/978-3-031-61308-1_5

H1: *There will be a significant and negative relationship between a self-protective leader who is self-centered and the effectiveness of a start-up business.*

B. **Status-Conscious Dimension of SPL**

Status-conscious leaders are highly aware of social positions and privileges. This awareness can positively influence leadership effectiveness by reducing social interaction stress and promoting a positive organizational image (Lipka & Brinthaupt, 1992).

H2: *There will be a significant and positive relationship between a self-protective leader who is status-conscious and the effectiveness of a start-up business.*

C. **Conflict-Inducer Dimension of SPL**

Conflict-inducing leaders promote competition among team members, driving innovation but also potentially causing friction. While this can foster creativity, it is generally viewed negatively in terms of global leadership effectiveness (House et al., 2004).

H3: *There will be a significant and negative relationship between a self-protective leader who is a conflict inducer and the effectiveness of a start-up business.*

D. **Face-Saving Dimension of SPL**

Face-saving leaders aim to prevent embarrassment among team members, maintaining positive relationships by avoiding negative comments. This behavior has a negligible effect on global leadership effectiveness (House et al., 2004).

H4: *There will be a significant and negative relationship between a self-protective leader who is a face-saver and the effectiveness of a start-up business.*

E. **Procedural Dimension of SPL**

Procedural leaders adhere strictly to established norms and routines. This attribute positively impacts leadership effectiveness by promoting consistency and efficiency (House et al., 2004).

H5: *There will be a significant and positive relationship between a self-protective leader who is bureaucratic and the effectiveness of a start-up business.*

F. **Strategic Entrepreneurial Behavior as a Moderator**

Strategic entrepreneurial behavior is expected to enhance the relationship between SPL attributes and start-up survival. It involves innovative actions that generate competitive advantages (Mazzei, 2018).

Moderating Hypotheses:

H6: *Strategic entrepreneurial behavior moderates the relationship between the self-conscious attribute of a self-protective leader and the effectiveness of a start-up business.*

H7: *Strategic entrepreneurial behavior moderates the relationship between the self-centered attribute of a self-protective leader and the effectiveness of a start-up business.*

H8: *Strategic entrepreneurial behavior moderates the relationship between the conflict-inducer attribute of a self-protective leader and the effectiveness of a start-up business.*

H9: *Strategic entrepreneurial behavior moderates the relationship between the face-saving attribute of a self-protective leader and the effectiveness of a start-up business.*

H10: *Strategic entrepreneurial behavior moderates the relationship between the bureaucratic attribute of a self-protective leader and the effectiveness of a start-up business.*

G. **Control Variables**

Control variables are factors that could influence the outcome of the study but are not the primary focus. By accounting for these variables, we can isolate the effect of the SPL attributes on start-up survival more accurately.

Market Dynamics

Market dynamics involve the forces that influence market prices and behaviors, such as supply and demand fluctuations, competitive actions, and human emotions affecting consumer behavior. These dynamics are crucial in understanding economic models and theories (Olaleye et al., 2020).

Technological Dynamics

Technological dynamics refer to the rapid introduction and integration of new technologies. Companies must foster creativity and take proactive measures to stay competitive in a technologically evolving world (Belderbos et al., 2019).

Market Uncertainty

Market uncertainty encompasses political, economic, and technological risks that affect business decisions and strategies. It can lead to difficulty in forecasting and maintaining a strategic advantage (Beckman et al., 2004).

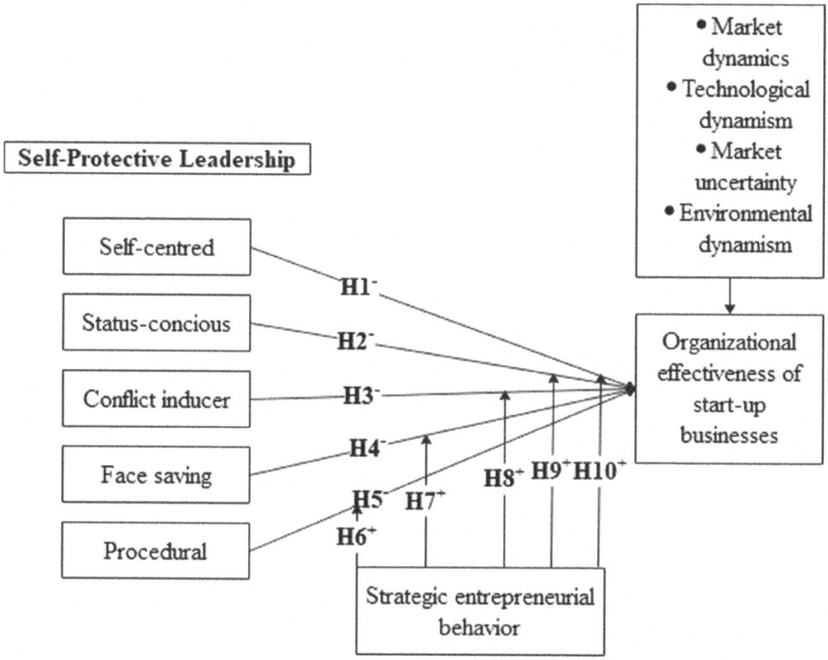

Fig. 5.1 Conceptual model and hypothesis development (*Source* Author)

Environmental Dynamics

Environmental dynamics describe the rate and unpredictability of changes in the environment, such as customer preferences and technological advancements. High environmental uncertainty can challenge firms in making informed decisions (Wijbenga & Van Witteloostuijn, 2007) (Fig. 5.1).

5.2 Results Summary

A summary of the key results is here displayed in Table 5.1

Table 5.1 Test of study hypotheses, summary

ID	Hypotheses	Kenya	Ghana
H1	*There will be a significant and negative relation between self-protective leader who is self-centered and the effectiveness of start-up business*	Not supported	**Supported**
H2	*There will be a significant and negative relation between self-protective leader who is self-conscious and the effectiveness of start-up business*	Not supported	Not supported
H3	*There will be a significant and negative relation between self-protective leader who is conflict inducer and the effectiveness of start-up business*	Not supported	**Supported**
H4	*There will be a significant and negative relation between self-protective leader who is face-saving and the effectiveness of start-up business*	Not supported	Not supported
H5	*There will be a significant and negative relation between self-protective leader who is procedural and the effectiveness of start-up business*	**Supported**	**Supported**
H6	*Strategic entrepreneurial behavior moderates the relation between self-centered leader and the effectiveness of start-up business*	**Supported**	**Supported**
H7	*Strategic entrepreneurial behavior moderates the relation between self-conscious attribute of a self-protective leader and the effectiveness of start-up business*	Not supported	Not supported
H8	*Strategic entrepreneurial behavior moderates the relation between conflict-inducer attribute of a self-protective leader and the effectiveness of start-up business*	Not supported	**Supported**

(continued)

Table 5.1 (continued)

ID	Hypotheses	Kenya	Ghana
H9	*Strategic entrepreneurial behavior moderates the relation between face-saver attribute of a self-protective leader and the effectiveness of start-up business*	Not supported	Not supported
H10	*Strategic entrepreneurial behavior moderates the relation between procedural attribute of a self-protective leader and the effectiveness of start-up business*	**Supported**	**Supported**

5.3 Discussion of Findings

The study aimed to explore the impact of self-protective leadership style on start-up businesses within the marketing communication industry in Africa, with a particular emphasis on how strategic entrepreneurial behavior moderates this relationship. Drawing on the Behavioral Theory of Leadership and Situational Leadership Theory, the research investigated various dimensions of self-protective leadership, including status-consciousness, face-saving behaviors, self-centeredness, conflict-inducement, and procedure-orientedness.

Ten hypotheses were formulated, each addressing different dimensions of the conceptual model. Five hypotheses focused on direct effects, while the remaining five examined moderating effects. The quantitative aspect of the study was conducted across two African countries: Ghana and Kenya. In Ghana, three out of the five direct hypotheses were supported, while in Kenya, only one out of the five direct hypotheses received support. Regarding the moderating hypotheses, three were supported in Ghana, whereas two were supported in Kenya.

The findings shed light on the complex interplay between self-protective leadership, strategic entrepreneurial behavior, and start-up business success within the African context. The empirical evidence presented offers valuable insights for practitioners and policymakers seeking to foster effective leadership strategies and promote entrepreneurial growth in the marketing communication industry in Africa.

A. Hypothesis 1 (H1): Self-Centered Leadership and Start-Up Business Survival

The findings regarding the first hypothesis, which examined the relationship between a self-protective leader who is self-centered and the organizational effectiveness of a start-up business, highlight the complexity of self-centeredness as a leadership dimension. The mixed results suggest that the impact of self-centered leadership on start-up business survival may vary depending on various contextual factors.

The supported aspect of the hypothesis indicates that in certain circumstances, self-centered leadership traits may indeed have a negative effect on the organizational effectiveness of start-up businesses. This could be attributed to self-centered leaders prioritizing their own interests over the collective goals of the organization, leading to decreased motivation and engagement among team members, as well as hindered collaboration and communication.

On the other hand, the unsupported aspect of the hypothesis suggests that there may be situations where self-centered leadership traits do not necessarily lead to negative outcomes for start-up businesses. In such cases, self-centered leaders may demonstrate assertiveness, confidence, and a drive for success, which could positively impact the organization's performance by driving innovation, decision-making, and goal achievement.

The quantitative findings regarding the first hypothesis reveal intriguing insights into the relationship between self-centered leadership and start-up business survival in Ghana and Kenya.

In Ghana, the study demonstrates a significant and negative relationship between self-centered leadership and the survival of start-up businesses. This suggests that self-centered leaders in Ghana may hinder the effectiveness and sustainability of start-up ventures. The adoption of an authoritarian management style and divergence from accepted organizational practices by self-centered leaders could potentially disrupt team dynamics, hinder collaboration, and impede organizational growth.

Conversely, in Kenya, the study shows a significant effect of self-centered leadership on the survival of start-up businesses, although the nature of this effect is not explicitly described. This indicates that self-centered leadership traits may have a different impact on start-up ventures in Kenya compared to Ghana. The reasons for this variation could be influenced by cultural, contextual, or organizational factors unique to each country.

The supporting evidence from Ghana aligns with previous research, such as the study by Kabasakal et al. (2012), which identified self-centered leadership as a common negative trait in certain regions, including the Middle East and North Africa (MENA) region. The association of self-centeredness with non-participative and socially detached attitudes further reinforces the idea that self-centered leadership may inhibit effective leadership practices and organizational outcomes.

In global business, Larry Ellison at Oracle provides a clear example of self-centered leadership that, despite its challenges, led to significant business achievements. Ellison's leadership, often described as authoritarian, was instrumental in driving Oracle's growth into one of the world's leading software companies. However, his focus on personal vision sometimes created a challenging work environment, highlighting the mixed outcomes of such leadership.

In contrast, Marissa Mayer's leadership at Yahoo presents a cautionary tale. Mayer, often criticized for her autocratic and self-centered style, struggled to turn Yahoo around, ultimately leading to the company's decline and sale to Verizon. Her leadership decisions, which were often seen as self-serving, alienated employees and failed to reinvigorate the company.

In Africa, Aliko Dangote's leadership of the Dangote Group illustrates how self-centered leadership can drive success. Dangote's personal vision and aggressive business strategies have transformed his company into a dominant force in the African industrial sector. While his leadership style has sometimes been criticized for being too centralized, his ability to align his personal goals with the company's growth objectives has been key to the conglomerate's success.

These examples illustrate that while self-centered leadership can drive success in certain contexts, particularly when combined with a strong vision and strategic acumen, it also carries significant risks that can lead to organizational failure if not carefully managed.

B. Hypothesis 2 (H2): Status-Conscious Leadership and Start-Up Business Survival

The quantitative findings regarding Hypothesis 2 reveal unexpected results concerning the relationship between status-conscious leadership and start-up business survival in both Kenya and Ghana.

Contrary to the hypothesis, the study indicates that status-conscious leaders have a significant and positive impact on the survival of start-up businesses in both countries. This suggests that leaders who are attentive to their status within the organization may contribute to the growth and success of start-up ventures.

The findings imply that the status-conscious attribute of leaders plays a beneficial role in fostering business growth and development. Leaders who are mindful of their status may exhibit behaviors that motivate and inspire their teams, cultivate a positive organizational culture, and establish strong relationships with stakeholders. Additionally, status-conscious leaders may be more attuned to market trends, competition, and strategic opportunities, enabling them to make informed decisions that drive business growth.

This unexpected outcome challenges conventional assumptions about the negative implications of status-conscious leadership and underscores the complexity of leadership dynamics in start-up environments. While status-consciousness may be perceived as a potential barrier to effective leadership, particularly in terms of fostering collaboration and teamwork, the findings suggest that in the context of start-up businesses, it may serve as a catalyst for success.

Furthermore, the outcome contrasts with some existing leadership theories that emphasize the role of entrepreneurial behavior in enhancing various leadership styles. While previous research, such as by Covin and Slevin (1989), suggests that entrepreneurial behavior is a key factor in business success, these findings highlight that in the case of status-conscious leadership, SEB might not always play a crucial role in moderating outcomes.

Howard Schultz's leadership at Starbucks showcases how status-conscious leadership can drive success without heavily relying on SEB. Schultz's focus on building Starbucks as a premium, high-status brand contributed to its global expansion. His leadership style leveraged the brand's social standing to fuel growth, though it was more about scaling the existing business model rather than driving new entrepreneurial initiatives.

In contrast, Richard Liu's leadership at JD.com in China illustrates how combining status-conscious leadership with SEB can be particularly effective. Liu's awareness of his status, along with his entrepreneurial drive, helped JD.com become a major player in China's e-commerce market. By leveraging his reputation and pursuing innovative logistics solutions, Liu positioned JD.com as a leader in its field.

In Africa, the leadership of Tony Elumelu at United Bank for Africa (UBA) and Heirs Holdings demonstrates how a leader's status-consciousness, when aligned with strategic entrepreneurial initiatives, can contribute to success. Elumelu's focus on his status and influence within the African business community, combined with his commitment to entrepreneurship through the Tony Elumelu Foundation, has been instrumental in driving growth and development across his ventures.

These cases indicate that while SEB is essential in many leadership contexts, its absence does not necessarily diminish the effectiveness of status-conscious leadership in ensuring start-up survival. In certain industries and cultural contexts, maintaining and leveraging status can be a sufficient strategy for business success.

C. Hypothesis 3 (H3): Conflict-Inducing Leadership and Start-Up Business Survival

The findings regarding Hypothesis 3 (H3) suggest interesting variations in the relationship between conflict-inducing leadership and start-up business survival in Ghana and Kenya.

In Ghana, the quantitative results indicate a significant and negative relationship between a self-protective leader who is a conflict inducer and the survival of start-up businesses. This implies that leaders who engage in conflict-inducing behaviors may detrimentally impact the effectiveness and longevity of start-up ventures in Ghana. The disruptive nature of conflict-inducing leadership could lead to decreased morale, increased turnover, and impaired team cohesion, ultimately hindering organizational success.

Conversely, in Kenya, the study findings reveal that the hypothesis was not supported, suggesting that conflict-inducing leadership had a significant and positive correlation with start-up businesses' survival. This unexpected result indicates that conflict-inducing behaviors by leaders may have a different impact on start-up ventures in Kenya compared to Ghana. The reasons for this variation could be influenced by cultural norms, organizational contexts, or other contextual factors unique to each country.

The findings from Ghana align with previous research by De Dreu & Gelfand (2008), which may provide additional support for the validity of the results. Understanding the detrimental effects of conflict-inducing leadership on start-up business survival underscores the importance of promoting constructive conflict resolution strategies and fostering positive interpersonal dynamics within organizational settings.

The outcome furthermore align partially with research by Tjosvold (2008), who argues that conflict, when managed correctly, can foster innovation and better decision-making. However, the absence of a moderating effect in Kenya suggests that SEB alone might not be sufficient to counteract the disruptive aspects of conflict-inducing leadership in certain environments.

Reed Hastings at Netflix exemplifies how conflict-inducing leadership, coupled with SEB, can lead to significant success. Hastings' leadership involved challenging the status quo and driving continuous innovation, even at the cost of internal conflict. His approach has transformed Netflix into a global leader in streaming services, demonstrating how conflict can be harnessed positively when combined with entrepreneurial strategies.

On the other hand, Adam Neumann's leadership at WeWork illustrates the risks of conflict-inducing leadership without effective SEB. Neumann's aggressive and often controversial leadership style led to rapid growth but ultimately resulted in a failed IPO and his ousting from the company. The absence of a clear, sustainable entrepreneurial strategy to balance the internal conflicts contributed to WeWork's downfall.

In Africa, the case of South Africa's Eskom under Brian Molefe highlights how conflict-inducing leadership can lead to organizational challenges. Molefe's tenure saw significant internal conflicts and controversial decisions that, combined with a lack of effective entrepreneurial strategies, exacerbated the utility's financial and operational crises.

These cases highlight the importance of managing conflict within organizations and suggest that while SEB can mitigate some negative effects, it is not a panacea. Effective leadership in start-ups requires a careful balance of conflict management and entrepreneurial strategy to drive innovation without compromising organizational cohesion.

D. **Hypothesis 4 (H4): Face-Saving Leadership and Start-Up Business Survival**

The findings related to Hypothesis 4 (H4) indicate that there was no significant and negative relationship between a self-protective leader who exhibits face-saving behaviors and the organizational effectiveness of start-up businesses in both Kenya and Ghana. Instead, the results suggest that the face-saving attributes of a leader may have a significant and positive impact on organizational effectiveness.

In essence, leaders who engage in face-saving behaviors, characterized by efforts to preserve their own or the organization's reputation and avoid embarrassment or loss of face, appear to contribute positively to the effectiveness of start-up businesses. This finding suggests that leaders who prioritize maintaining a positive image and reputation, both personally and for the organization, may foster a more conducive work environment conducive to success.

The absence of a significant negative relationship contradicts the initial expectation that face-saving behaviors, which may involve avoiding accountability or withholding information to protect one's image, could hinder organizational effectiveness. However, the results suggest that in the context of start-up businesses in Kenya and Ghana, such behaviors may not have the anticipated detrimental effects.

This finding underscores the complexity of leadership dynamics and the need to consider contextual factors when assessing their impact on organizational outcomes. It also suggests that certain leadership behaviors, such as face-saving, may manifest differently in different cultural or organizational contexts, potentially yielding varying effects on organizational effectiveness.

Moreover, the results challenge the traditional view that face-saving leadership is inherently negative. Previous studies, like those by Ting-Toomey (1994), have often criticized face-saving behaviors for promoting a lack of transparency and hindering effective communication. However, the findings here suggest that in the context of start-ups, especially in cultures where maintaining face is important, these behaviors might help preserve relationships and social harmony, which are crucial for business success.

In the global context, the leadership style of Hiroshi Mikitani at Rakuten offers an example of face-saving practices being integrated into a broader strategy for business success. Mikitani, while implementing a challenging English-only policy at Rakuten, also made efforts to save face for employees by providing extensive support and training. This approach helped maintain employee morale while driving the company's global expansion.

Another example is that of Toyota's leadership during the 2010 recall crisis. The company's leaders initially engaged in face-saving behaviors by downplaying the severity of the issues. However, once the crisis escalated, they shifted to a more transparent approach, balancing the need to save face with the necessity of addressing the problem. This strategy helped Toyota recover its reputation and maintain its market position.

In Africa, the leadership of Nigeria's Access Bank during its merger with Diamond Bank demonstrates how face-saving behaviors can be effectively managed. The merger was handled in a way that respected the dignity and reputation of both organizations, which helped facilitate a smooth integration process and preserved stakeholder confidence.

These examples show that while face-saving leadership can have drawbacks, it can also play a role in maintaining organizational stability and relationships, especially in cultures that value harmony and respect. The key is to balance face-saving with transparency and accountability to ensure that it does not impede organizational effectiveness.

E. **Hypothesis 5 (H5): Procedural Leadership and Start-Up Business Survival**

Hypothesis 5 (H5) posited that there would be a significant and negative relationship between a self-protective leader who is procedural and the organizational effectiveness of a start-up business. This hypothesis was supported by the quantitative results obtained from both Kenya and Ghana.

The findings suggest that leaders who exhibit procedural tendencies, characterized by a focus on following established processes and protocols methodically, have a significant negative impact on the organizational effectiveness of start-up businesses in both countries. This implies that a strict adherence to procedures may hinder rather than enhance the effectiveness of start-up organizations.

The negative relationship between procedural leadership and organizational effectiveness may be attributed to several factors. First, excessive rigidity and inflexibility in following procedures may stifle innovation and adaptability, limiting the organization's ability to respond effectively to changing market conditions or emerging opportunities.

Second, a procedural leadership style may lead to bureaucratic inefficiencies and delays, hindering the organization's agility and responsiveness. Start-up businesses often require quick decision-making and nimble operations to capitalize on market opportunities and overcome challenges, and excessive proceduralism may impede these efforts. Additionally, a focus on procedural adherence may detract leaders from more strategic or visionary aspects of leadership, such as fostering innovation, building strong relationships with stakeholders, or cultivating a dynamic organizational culture. This could result in missed opportunities for growth and development.

This outcome is in many respects consistent with existing leadership theories that emphasize the limitations of procedural leadership in dynamic environments. For instance, the GLOBE study (House et al., 2004) highlights how procedural leadership can be counterproductive in rapidly changing markets, where flexibility and innovation are essential. Similarly, studies by Eisenhardt and Martin (2000) have shown that in high-velocity environments, excessive proceduralism can lead to rigidity, preventing organizations from adapting to new challenges and opportunities effectively. The findings from this study reinforce the idea that while procedures provide structure, they can also impede the creativity and responsiveness necessary for start-up success.

A case that exemplifies the pitfalls of procedural leadership is the decline of BlackBerry. Once a dominant player in the smartphone market, BlackBerry's leadership maintained a rigid adherence to its established operating system and physical keyboard design, even as consumer preferences shifted toward touchscreens and app-based ecosystems. The company's failure to innovate and adapt quickly to these changes, due to its procedural rigidity, led to a rapid decline in market share and relevance, ultimately resulting in BlackBerry's exit from the consumer smartphone market.

In contrast, the leadership of Satya Nadella at Microsoft illustrates the effective combination of procedural leadership with strategic entrepreneurial behavior (SEB). When Nadella became CEO, he inherited a company known for its procedural approach to product development and operations. However, Nadella introduced a culture of innovation, focusing on cloud computing and artificial intelligence, which allowed Microsoft to regain its competitive edge. His leadership demonstrated how procedural structure, when combined with a strategic entrepreneurial mindset, can lead to significant growth and transformation.

In Africa, the leadership of Maria Ramos at Absa Group (formerly Barclays Africa) provides a compelling example of balancing procedural leadership with SEB. Ramos implemented robust procedures and governance structures essential for managing operations across multiple African countries. Simultaneously, she led strategic initiatives such as Absa's separation from Barclays and its rebranding, positioning the group as a distinctly African financial services provider. This strategic entrepreneurial approach, combined with procedural discipline, was key to navigating regulatory challenges and seizing new market opportunities.

These cases illustrate that while procedural leadership offers necessary structure, it must be balanced with strategic entrepreneurial behavior to foster innovation and adaptability. Leaders who integrate these approaches can drive both stability and growth, ensuring long-term success in today's competitive business environments.

F. Hypothesis 6 (H6): SEB as a Moderator Between Self-Centered Leadership and Organizational Effectiveness

Hypothesis 6 (H6) proposed that strategic entrepreneurial behavior (SEB) moderates the relationship between self-centered characteristics of a self-protective leadership style and the survival of start-up businesses. The quantitative results supported this hypothesis, indicating that strategic entrepreneurial behavior plays a moderating role in strengthening this relationship positively.

The findings suggest that when leaders exhibit self-centered characteristics as part of a self-protective leadership style, strategic entrepreneurial behavior can enhance the survival prospects of start-up businesses. Strategic entrepreneurial behavior involves proactive and innovative actions aimed at identifying and exploiting opportunities to create value and gain competitive advantage.

In the context of self-protective leadership, strategic entrepreneurial behavior enables leaders to personalize their approach to work and leverage entrepreneurial strategies to create opportunities within the business. By adopting a mindset focused on innovation and creativity, self-protective leaders can develop novel solutions to challenges, explore new markets, and pioneer disruptive initiatives that contribute to the sustainability and growth of start-up businesses.

Furthermore, the results suggest that self-protective leaders who view the organization as their own are motivated to implement creative and innovative management practices that align with strategic entrepreneurial behavior. This proactive approach to leadership enables them to capitalize on opportunities, mitigate risks, and adapt to changing market dynamics, thereby enhancing the effectiveness and survival prospects of start-up businesses.

This finding aligns with earlier research by Covin and Slevin (1989), which emphasized the role of entrepreneurial orientation in enhancing leadership effectiveness. SEB allows self-centered leaders to focus their personal ambitions on innovative strategies that benefit the organization, thus mitigating potential negative effects of their leadership style.

Elon Musk's leadership at Tesla and SpaceX provides a compelling example of this dynamic. Musk's leadership style is often described as self-centered, with a strong focus on his personal vision. However, his entrepreneurial drive and ability to innovate have been key to the success of both companies. Musk's relentless pursuit of his goals has led to groundbreaking achievements in electric vehicles and space exploration, demonstrating how SEB can channel self-centered leadership into positive outcomes.

In contrast, the leadership of Travis Kalanick at Uber highlights the risks of self-centered leadership without effective SEB. Kalanick's aggressive and often controversial leadership style drove Uber's rapid growth, but it also led to numerous legal and ethical issues. His failure to balance personal ambition with sustainable entrepreneurial strategies ultimately resulted in his departure from the company.

In Africa, the case of Strive Masiyiwa at Econet Wireless illustrates how self-centered leadership, when aligned with SEB, can drive success. Masiyiwa's determination to build a telecommunications network in Zimbabwe, despite significant challenges, reflects his strong personal drive. His entrepreneurial strategies, including securing international funding and leveraging innovative technologies, were critical in establishing Econet as a leading telecom provider in Africa.

These cases underscore the importance of SEB in enhancing the positive aspects of self-centered leadership. By aligning personal ambitions with strategic goals, leaders can drive innovation and organizational success while mitigating the potential downsides of a self-centered approach.

G. **Hypothesis 7 (H7): SEB as a Moderator Between Status-Conscious Leadership and Organizational Effectiveness**

Hypothesis 7 (H7) aimed to investigate whether strategic entrepreneurial behavior moderates the relationship between the status-conscious attribute of a self-protective leader and the survival of start-up businesses. However, the quantitative analysis results did not support this hypothesis, suggesting that strategic entrepreneurial behavior does not strengthen this relationship.

The findings indicate that the role of strategic entrepreneurial behavior does not have a significant impact on the relationship between a leader's status-conscious attribute and the survival of start-up businesses. This implies that even if a leader is highly concerned with their social status within the organization, strategic entrepreneurial behavior does not enhance the effectiveness of their leadership in terms of ensuring the survival and success of the start-up business.

The lack of support for Hypothesis 7 suggests that leaders who are overly focused on their social status may not be effectively leveraging strategic entrepreneurial behavior to seek and capitalize on opportunities for the benefit of the organization. Instead, their preoccupation with status-related concerns may distract them from identifying and pursuing initiatives that could enhance the performance and sustainability of the start-up business.

Furthermore, the findings suggest that leaders who prioritize their social status may be less inclined to engage in proactive and innovative behaviors associated with strategic entrepreneurship. As a result, they may miss out on opportunities for growth and fail to effectively address challenges facing the start-up business, ultimately reducing its long-term organizational effectiveness.

This outcome contrasts with some existing leadership theories, such as those proposed by House and Aditya (1997), which suggest that entrepreneurial behavior enhances the effectiveness of various leadership styles. The findings here imply that in the case of status-conscious leadership, SEB might not be as critical, and that other factors may play a more significant role in determining start-up success.

A case in point is the leadership of Sheryl Sandberg at Facebook, where her status-conscious leadership has played a role in her success as Chief Operating Officer (COO). Sandberg's emphasis on her professional reputation and status within the tech industry has helped her drive significant growth at Facebook. However, this success has been more about scaling existing initiatives rather than introducing radically new entrepreneurial strategies.

On the other hand, the leadership of Sir Martin Sorrell at WPP illustrates how status-conscious leadership, when paired with SEB, can lead to global dominance. Sorrell's focus on his status and reputation within the advertising industry, combined with his strategic acquisitions and innovative business models, helped WPP become the world's largest advertising company.

In Africa, Koos Bekker's leadership at Naspers demonstrates how a leader's status-conscious approach, combined with entrepreneurial innovation, can transform a company. Bekker's ability to leverage his reputation and status in the media industry, while also pioneering investments in emerging markets like China (e.g., Tencent), has been crucial to Naspers' success as a global media giant.

These cases suggest that while SEB can enhance leadership effectiveness in some contexts, it may not always be necessary for status-conscious leaders to succeed. In some instances, leveraging social standing and existing business models may be sufficient for driving growth and ensuring the survival of start-ups.

H. **Hypothesis 8 (H8): SEB as a Moderator Between Conflict-Inducing Leadership and Organizational Effectiveness**

Hypothesis 8 (H8) proposed that strategic entrepreneurial behavior moderates the relationship between the conflict-inducing attribute of a self-protective leader and the organizational effectiveness of a start-up business. The hypothesis yielded mixed results, being supported for Ghana but not for Kenya, suggesting a divergence in findings between the two countries.

In the context of conflict-inducing leadership, which involves behaviors that lead to interpersonal conflicts within the organization, strategic entrepreneurial behavior was expected to mitigate the negative impact of such leadership on the organizational effectiveness of start-up businesses.

The quantitative analysis supported this hypothesis for Ghana, indicating that strategic entrepreneurial behavior plays a moderating role in strengthening the relationship between conflict-inducing leadership and the survival of start-up businesses. This suggests that in Ghana, strategic entrepreneurial behavior can help offset the detrimental effects of conflict-inducing leadership by fostering innovation, collaboration, and problem-solving within the organization.

However, the hypothesis was not supported for Kenya, indicating that strategic entrepreneurial behavior did not significantly influence the relationship between conflict-inducing leadership and the organizational effectiveness of start-up businesses in this context. This suggests that other factors may be more influential in shaping the outcomes of conflict-inducing leadership in Kenyan start-up businesses.

The contrasting findings between Ghana and Kenya underscore the importance of considering contextual factors and cultural differences when examining the relationship between leadership styles, entrepreneurial behavior, and organizational effectiveness. While strategic entrepreneurial behavior may be effective in mitigating the negative effects of conflict-inducing leadership in one context, its impact may vary in different cultural and organizational settings.

This result aligns with the work of De Dreu and Weingart (2003), who found that conflict can be beneficial when it stimulates innovation and problem-solving. However, the variation between Ghana and Kenya suggests that cultural and contextual factors play a significant role in how conflict and SEB interact within organizations.

The case of Steve Jobs at Apple is an example of how conflict-inducing leadership, when combined with SEB, can lead to significant innovation. Jobs was known for his confrontational style, often pushing his teams to their limits. However, his entrepreneurial vision and drive for perfection led to groundbreaking products like the iPhone, which revolutionized the tech industry.

Conversely, the leadership of John Sculley at Apple after Jobs' initial departure highlights the risks of conflict-inducing leadership without effective SEB. Sculley's tenure saw internal conflicts but lacked the entrepreneurial drive to push the company forward, leading to a period of stagnation for Apple.

In Africa, the leadership of Robert Gumede at Gijima Group provides a relevant example. Gumede's leadership style was marked by a willingness to engage in conflict, particularly in challenging the status quo within the IT industry. His entrepreneurial strategies, including aggressive acquisitions and expansion into new markets, helped establish

Gijima as a leading IT company in South Africa, despite the challenges posed by his leadership style.

These cases highlight the importance of balancing conflict-inducing leadership with strategic entrepreneurial behavior. While conflict can drive innovation, it needs to be channeled through effective entrepreneurial strategies to ensure it contributes to the survival and success of start-ups.

I. Hypothesis 9 (H9): SEB as a Moderator Between Face-Saving Leadership and Organizational Effectiveness

Hypothesis 9 (H9) posited that strategic entrepreneurial behavior moderates the relationship between the face-saving attribute of a self-protective leader and the survival of start-up businesses. However, the hypothesis was not supported in both Ghana and Kenya, indicating that strategic entrepreneurial behavior did not significantly influence the relationship between face-saving leadership and the survival of start-up businesses in either country.

The findings suggest that the tendency of self-protective leaders to engage in face-saving behaviors, which involve efforts to protect their own reputation and avoid humiliation, may limit their willingness to adopt strategic entrepreneurial behavior. Face-saving leaders may prioritize maintaining their image and avoiding risks, rather than pursuing innovative or entrepreneurial opportunities that could benefit the organization.

In this context, leaders who are focused on face-saving may be less inclined to take risks or explore new ventures, which could ultimately hinder the growth and survival of start-up businesses. Their reluctance to embrace strategic entrepreneurial behavior may limit the organization's ability to adapt to changing market conditions, identify new opportunities, and effectively compete in the marketplace.

The implications of these findings highlight the importance of understanding the impact of leadership behaviors on organizational outcomes, particularly in the context of start-up businesses where innovation and adaptation are critical for success. Leaders who prioritize face-saving may need to be encouraged or incentivized to embrace strategic entrepreneurial behavior, recognizing the potential benefits it can bring to the organization's long-term viability and competitiveness.

The results nonetheless contrast with earlier research by Leung and Kim (2007), which highlighted the importance of face-saving in high-context cultures where maintaining relationships and social harmony is crucial. However, the findings here suggest that in the context of start-ups, particularly in the dynamic environments of Ghana and Kenya, face-saving alone does not significantly influence survival when not paired with strong entrepreneurial actions.

In Japan, the leadership of Masayoshi Son at SoftBank provides an interesting contrast. Son's leadership style, while respectful of Japanese cultural norms around face-saving, has also been heavily entrepreneurial. His aggressive investment strategies, particularly in the tech sector, have driven SoftBank's global expansion. Son's ability to balance face-saving with entrepreneurial risk-taking has been key to SoftBank's success.

Another example is the leadership of Carlos Ghosn at Nissan-Renault, where face-saving behaviors were initially used to navigate the complex cultural dynamics between French and Japanese partners. However, Ghosn's failure to maintain transparency and accountability ultimately led to his downfall, demonstrating the limitations of face-saving when not combined with effective entrepreneurial leadership.

In Africa, the leadership of James Mwangi at Equity Bank Kenya illustrates how face-saving behaviors can be effectively managed in conjunction with SEB. Mwangi's respectful approach to managing relationships within the bank and with external stakeholders has been crucial in maintaining trust and social harmony. At the same time, his entrepreneurial initiatives, such as the introduction of mobile banking, have driven Equity Bank's growth and success in the region.

These cases demonstrate that while face-saving behaviors can help maintain social harmony and relationships, they need to be complemented by strong entrepreneurial strategies to drive start-up success, particularly in dynamic and competitive markets.

J. Hypothesis 10 (H10): SEB as a Moderator Between Procedural Leadership and Organizational Effectiveness

Hypothesis 10 (H10) posited that strategic entrepreneurial behavior moderates the relationship between the procedural attribute of a self-protective leader and the survival of start-up businesses. The hypothesis was supported in both Ghana and Kenya, indicating that strategic entrepreneurial behavior has a significant moderating effect on the relationship between procedural leadership and the survival of start-up businesses in both countries.

The findings suggest that in start-up organizations, leaders who exhibit procedural leadership styles may benefit from incorporating strategic entrepreneurial behavior into their approach. Procedural leaders typically emphasize following established protocols and procedures to ensure efficiency and consistency in operations. However, by embracing strategic entrepreneurial behavior, these leaders can foster a culture of innovation and creativity within the organization, which can contribute to the long-term survival and success of the business.

Strategic entrepreneurial behavior allows leaders to encourage employees to contribute ideas and suggestions for improving processes and operations, thereby enhancing organizational effectiveness and adaptability. By leveraging the procedural attributes of self-protective leaders and combining them with strategic entrepreneurial behavior, start-up businesses can create a conducive environment for innovation and growth while still maintaining the discipline and structure necessary for efficient operations.

The implication of these findings is that organizations led by self-protective leaders with procedural tendencies can enhance their chances of survival and success by embracing strategic entrepreneurial behavior. This involves not only adhering to established procedures but also actively seeking out opportunities for innovation and improvement, and empowering employees to contribute to the organization's growth and development.

This finding aligns with the work of Fayol (1916) and later by Mintzberg (1973), who emphasized the importance of combining formal processes with strategic initiatives. The ability to maintain order while also pursuing new opportunities is crucial for the long-term success of start-ups.

Satya Nadella's leadership at Microsoft is an example of procedural leadership combined with SEB. Nadella's focus on process improvement and operational efficiency has been complemented by his entrepreneurial push into cloud computing and AI, transforming Microsoft into a leading tech company in these fields.

On the contrary, the leadership of Marissa Mayer at Yahoo demonstrates the risks of procedural leadership without effective strategic entrepreneurial behavior (SEB). Mayer implemented several procedural changes to streamline operations at Yahoo, but her failure to effectively innovate and adapt to the rapidly changing tech landscape led to the company's decline. Despite her efforts to maintain order and structure, the lack of a clear, innovative strategy ultimately resulted in Yahoo being sold to Verizon at a significant loss.

In Africa, Maria Ramos' leadership at Absa Group (formerly Barclays Africa) highlights the effective combination of procedural leadership with SEB. Ramos focused on establishing robust procedures and governance structures within Absa, which were essential for managing the complexities of operating across multiple African countries. Concurrently, she drove strategic initiatives such as the bank's separation from Barclays and its rebranding as Absa, positioning the group as a distinctly African financial services provider. This blend of procedural leadership with strategic entrepreneurship was key to navigating regulatory challenges and seizing new market opportunities.

These examples illustrate that while procedural leadership provides the necessary structure and consistency for operations, it is the integration of strategic entrepreneurial behavior that allows start-ups and established companies alike to innovate, adapt, and thrive in competitive environments. Leaders who successfully balance these elements can drive both stability and growth, ensuring long-term organizational success.

5.4 Case Study of Ghana's Advertising Industry

Methodological Design

In this case study, we used a qualitative approach to understand the impact of self-protective leadership on start-up businesses within Ghana's marketing communication industry. Case studies, defined by Creswell (2014) and Creswell and Piano Clark (2007), involve observing contemporary events within their natural environment and are widely recognized for providing comprehensive insights into organizational dynamics and social phenomena.

The research aimed to assess how self-protective leadership influences start-ups, considering the role of strategic entrepreneurial behavior. We selected 13 leaders from start-up ventures in the marketing communication sector to gather a diverse range of perspectives. An interview guide with ten questions was developed, and respondents were provided with these questions a week in advance to facilitate preparation. During interviews, we recorded and transcribed responses, ensuring detailed capture of their views.

By focusing on real-life operational and administrative processes, this case study offered valuable insights into the practical challenges of self-protective leadership in start-ups. Our approach provided a structured framework for observation and contributed to a deeper understanding of leadership dynamics within this specific context, with potential implications for future research and policy development.

Presentation of Findings

Our study delved into elucidating the impact, advantages, and drawbacks associated with employing the self-protective leadership style. By examining the perspectives of institutional and organizational leaders within the start-up business realm, we aimed to offer valuable insights into this leadership approach.

Based on the viewpoints of our respondents, the subsequent sections of our findings shed light on the benefits and opportunities linked with the adoption of self-protective leadership. Additionally, we addressed some of the challenges inherent in its implementation.

Furthermore, our research delved into exploring the effects of self-protective leadership on organizational effectiveness, providing a comprehensive analysis of its influence within this context. Through this examination, we aimed to provide a nuanced understanding of the implications of this leadership style on the overall performance and success of start-up ventures.

A. **Benefits and Opportunities Associated with the SPL Style**

Organizational leaders within start-up businesses often opt for the self-protective leadership style to effectively manage the daily operations of their organizations. While previous studies primarily focused on elucidating the effects of alternative leadership styles, our research uniquely investigates the impact of self-protective leadership on start-up ventures, exploring both the opportunities and challenges associated with its implementation.

Our findings revealed that leaders who embrace the self-protective approach experience numerous benefits and opportunities. By embodying this style, leaders reported enhanced business growth, the cultivation of trust and admiration among clients, and a heightened assurance in the quality of their products or services. Additionally, the self-protective stance helped leaders safeguard themselves from potential financial liabilities, thereby contributing to the sustainability of their businesses.

Participants in our case study shared their perspectives on the matter. One participant expressed:

> First of all, it enabled me to build a solid ground, it also allowed me to win the admiration of most of my clients I have today, and also assured me of the product I have executed in the past that they are of the best quality, and I have not been dragged into any financial debt because I was protective enough to save myself from any of such occurrences.

Overall, our research underscores the valuable role of self-protective leadership in driving success and sustainability within start-up businesses, offering a compelling rationale for its adoption by organizational leaders.

This implies that adopting a self-protective leadership style enables you to guide your start-up business in a manner that garners admiration from customers within your industry. It also ensures that employees within the start-up are able to adhere to production processes effectively, thereby guaranteeing the delivery of high-quality products or services.

One participant articulated this sentiment, stating:

> I think with me, this will help bring stability and reliability to the business because I have done too many businesses that have failed, because I haven't looked out for myself enough and protected the business enough, so I think in the long term, ultimately this kind of leadership will ensure that I leave a legacy or a business that is attractive to investors to come in. Therefore, with a clear direction, focus, being in charge and control of where this business is going, I believe that the business is well structured.

In essence, being a self-protective leader not only fosters stability and reliability within your business but also lays the groundwork for leaving a lasting legacy and attracting potential investors. Through clear direction, focus, and effective control, self-protective leadership ensures the structured growth and success of the business in the long run.

Similarly, the respondent's statement regarding the opportunities and benefits associated with the use of self-protective leadership underscores the crucial role of this leadership style in safeguarding both the leader and the organization they have built. By adopting a self-protective approach, leaders can effectively protect their business interests, thereby ensuring the organizational effectiveness of the start-up venture. This entails the leader taking charge and maintaining control over the direction of the business, providing clear directives, and remaining focused to uphold its stability and reliability.

As aptly illustrated by the respondent:

> A popular Akan proverb says, when you pluck hair from your nostrils you are the one who feels the pain, therefore the benefit of a self-protective

> leader is that it helps you to monitor your workers and make sure your interest is protected and without that the company can't survive.

This proverb highlights the fundamental principle that self-protection is essential for survival. In the context of leadership, a self-protective approach empowers leaders to oversee their workforce and safeguard their own interests, thereby ensuring the viability and longevity of the company. The statement moreover underscores the importance of self-protective leadership in ensuring the effectiveness and growth of a start-up business. By employing this leadership style, organizational leaders can keep employees engaged and motivated, thereby driving productivity and adherence to proper procedures throughout the production process. The procedural and conflict inducer dimensions of self-protective leadership serve to maintain a sense of urgency and accountability among employees, ultimately contributing to the organization's future success.

As one participant articulated:

> I think for me the advantages are that it keeps the business moving, because I started the business and I know where my target is, so anyone who comes in as an employee must basically follow my lead, since the goal is to ensure that people are not doing things that might affect the business in a negative way. I have learnt over the years that when it comes to business, when there is a problem, employees quit and leave without looking back so even though I care about employee's welfare, I ultimately want to ensure that my business thrives with or without them.

This perspective highlights the need for proactive leadership to steer the business toward its objectives, while also emphasizing the importance of maintaining a cohesive and focused workforce.

Similarly, another participant shared their viewpoint, stating:

> I think the obvious benefit will be that if you involve yourself in all aspects of the business you will have a better chance of managing it properly, and it helps you understand all aspects of the business and helps you do better.

This perspective underscores the value of hands-on involvement by leaders in all facets of the business, enabling a comprehensive understanding of its operations and facilitating effective management practices.

In essence, the adoption of self-protective leadership not only ensures the business's operational efficiency but also fosters a culture of accountability and dedication among employees, ultimately positioning the organization for sustained growth and success.

The self-protective leader, being deeply involved in steering the business toward its goals, engages comprehensively in all aspects and ongoing improvements within the organization. This active involvement provides the leader with a wealth of data and information crucial for making informed decisions and spearheading initiatives aimed at advancing the organization's objectives. By immersing themselves in various aspects of the business, the leader gains insights that facilitate prioritization of activities, meeting deadlines, and devising innovative approaches to operations. This proactive approach not only ensures the stability of the business but also fosters its organizational effectiveness.

As one participant aptly put it:

> Firstly, it's to give the owner the assurance that your business will not be stolen away, secondly, it helps you to be defensive in terms of staff connivance with other parties and grinding your business to a halt, and finally it gives you a peace of mind knowing that your business is carefully guided and protected.

This perspective highlights the multifaceted benefits of self-protective leadership. It serves as a safeguard against potential threats such as theft or collusion, providing the leader with a sense of security and confidence in the careful guidance and protection of their business.

Furthermore, the use of a self-protective leadership style within an organization presents opportunities for leaders to safeguard their businesses and ensure that employees are aligned with the leaders' objectives for the business.

In summary, our study findings regarding the benefits and opportunities associated with self-protective leadership style suggest that effective implementation of this approach can significantly contribute to driving organizational success. Essentially, self-protective leadership offers opportunities and benefits that pave the way for business success. This sentiment was echoed by respondents through the following statements:

1. *If self-protective leadership is practiced right, it allows you to build solid systems that ensure growth, better and faster.*
2. *All I can say is if you are not a self-protective leader, your company can't survive, so the benefit would be that your company will grow.*

B. **Challenges with the SPL Style**

When a leader adopts the self-protective leadership style to manage their business affairs, several difficulties may arise, as highlighted in the findings of this study. While the benefits of this leadership style were previously outlined, it's essential to recognize its inherent shortcomings, which, if left unaddressed, could potentially undermine the success of the start-up business.

One notable challenge associated with the use of self-protective leadership style is the toll of exhaustion and stress placed on the leader. Given that they bear sole responsibility for managing the business, leaders may find themselves constantly on duty, leading to burnout and heightened stress levels. Additionally, the burden of decision-making resting solely on one individual can be overwhelming.

Participants in the study shared their perspectives on these challenges. One respondent articulated:

> The challenge is, you are the only person running the business and the question is, can you be there around the clock, leading to exhaustion and stress. Again, you might wish to have someone you can trust to leave the company in his care and have some time for yourself.

In essence, while self-protective leadership offers certain advantages, it also poses significant challenges, such as exhaustion, stress, and the weight of sole decision-making responsibility. Addressing these challenges is crucial for sustaining the effectiveness and longevity of the start-up business.

Self-protective leaders, often perceived as solitary figures, tend to shoulder the responsibilities of their organizations single-handedly, eschewing support from others. Their relentless pursuit of omnipresence within the organization can lead to exhaustion and ultimately render their leadership ineffective. This strain on the leader can have detrimental effects on the overall effectiveness of a start-up business. Managing as a self-protective leader is inherently time-consuming, and without the capacity to delegate, exhaustion and stress are inevitable, particularly in start-ups with sizable workforces exceeding 100 employees.

However, amidst these challenges, one respondent proposed a potential solution: the gradual cultivation of trust between managers and employees. This trust would empower the manager to entrust key responsibilities to capable employees, ensuring the smooth operation of the business even in their absence. Reflecting on this possibility, the respondent remarked:

> It's not easy, and you can't always trust Ghanaian workers outright. However, over time, you may identify a few individuals whom you could rely on, albeit with vigilance. Building trust with workers can be fostered by fair compensation and fostering positive relationships, which in turn may encourage diligence.

The respondent also highlighted the cultural dynamics at play, noting:

> I don't know if it's a cultural thing, but many individuals feel entitled. They join the business and quickly seek increased compensation and influence over its direction. If their aspirations align with my vision, persuasion may be effective, but misalignment often leads to departure. In the long run, I anticipate attracting individuals who share my business ethos.

The statement above highlights a significant challenge associated with the self-protective leadership style, as articulated by one of the respondents. This leadership approach often results in a high turnover of employees within an organization. When leaders exhibit or are perceived to embody self-protective behaviors, it fosters an atmosphere of mistrust between them and their employees. Consequently, collaborative efforts become strained, making it difficult for teams to work cohesively.

Furthermore, in their efforts to safeguard their own interests within the organization, leaders may react harshly to any perceived threats or challenges posed by employees. This could lead to disciplinary actions or even the dismissal of employees who are viewed as obstacles to the leader's objectives. Such practices contribute to a revolving door of talent within the organization. If leaders fail to promptly replace departing employees, it can significantly hamper the effectiveness of the start-up business.

As one respondent eloquently put it:

> Employees who are very laborious in nature become very uncomfortable within such environments, and the likelihood of resignation is very high. Secondly, the issue of conclusive authority is not guaranteed in any of the employees, preventing them from working independently and making decisions without seeking approval.

In alignment with this sentiment, the adoption of a self-protective leadership style often results in employees feeling disconnected from the organization. This lack of a sense of belonging translates into diminished willingness and commitment to their roles. Consequently, tasks may remain unfinished, deadlines may be missed, and overall job satisfaction and customer service quality may suffer within the organization.

These insights, drawn from the experiences shared by the interviewees, underscore the detrimental effects of employing a self-protective leadership style, particularly within the context of a start-up business.

C. **Impact of the SPL Style on Start-Up Businesses**

The primary objective of this study was to evaluate the implications of employing a self-protective leadership style within a start-up business operating in the marketing communications industry. Through gathering opinions and perspectives from the respondents, insights were gained into the potential effects of this leadership approach on the day-to-day operations of such businesses.

Participants offered varied opinions regarding the impact of the self-protective leadership style, with some acknowledging its dual nature—both beneficial and detrimental. While a few respondents highlighted potential drawbacks, such as feelings of being micromanaged and a lack of trust among staff, the majority expressed a belief in its positive influence on organizational effectiveness within start-up ventures.

One respondent aptly captured this perspective by stating:

> It could be a double-edged sword because it could have a negative effect on staff, with some feeling micromanaged and lacking trust in their abilities to perform their duties. For instance, in one company, 23 workers felt compelled to resign due to perceived mistreatment. As a self-protective leader, one risks becoming overly fixated on the success of the business, which poses its own set of risks.

This viewpoint underscores the delicate balance that self-protective leaders must navigate between driving business success and maintaining a supportive and trusting work environment. While the potential for positive outcomes exists, it is essential for leaders to be mindful of the potential pitfalls associated with this leadership style, particularly concerning employee morale and retention.

Therefore, it becomes evident that while the self-protective leadership style can contribute to the success of a business, an excessive focus on company achievements may result in a lack of adequate attention to employee welfare. The feedback provided by respondents underscores the dual nature of this leadership approach within start-up businesses—it can have both positive impacts and negative consequences on organizational effectiveness.

Hence, leaders contemplating the adoption of a self-protective leadership style must strike a balance to avoid neglecting the welfare of their employees. Recognizing that employee well-being is integral to long-term success, leaders should prioritize managing this leadership approach effectively.

As one respondent emphasized:

> I believe employees seek stability in a business and leaders who can lead them toward success. When employees perceive that a leader can guide them to achieve their goals, they are more inclined to invest maximum effort. Ultimately, it's not about personal interests but rather the growth and survival of the business. Additionally, as the leader, I understand the responsibility of ensuring the business's success, even if it means adopting an autocratic approach at times. Employees will align with this approach when they recognize its alignment with the interests of the business.

This sentiment highlights the importance of fostering a shared vision of organizational success while acknowledging the leader's responsibility to steer the business through challenges. By striking a balance between prioritizing the company's interests and ensuring employee welfare, leaders can effectively leverage the self-protective leadership style to drive the growth and success of their start-up ventures.

This suggests that the implementation of self-protective leadership can indeed yield positive outcomes for start-up businesses. In organizations where the head employs a self-protective leadership approach aimed at fostering business growth while assuring job security for employees, a positive impact is observed. This strategy effectively motivates employees to strive for excellence and contribute toward achieving the organization's goals.

For instance, as one respondent noted:

> I believe for a startup business, self-protective leadership is paramount. Starting any business is challenging, and adopting any other leadership style might lead to easily giving up. However, self-protective leadership offers advantages by driving the business to a certain level before considering different management styles.

Another respondent highlighted the effectiveness of self-protective leadership when properly utilized, stating:

> It can be effective when used properly because it makes you more resilient. For instance, I started this business five years ago, and during this time, we encountered various challenges such as staff turnover, unpaid invoices, and misunderstanding among employees. However, these challenges

> provided opportunities for system development and transformational leadership. Self-protective leadership acts as a catalyst for transformation.

From the perspective of the respondents, there is unanimous agreement on the positive impact of adopting self-protective leadership in start-up businesses. Given that leaders in start-up ventures often double as entrepreneurs, employing self-protective leadership aids in achieving desired objectives—ensuring organizational effectiveness and long-term stability.

Thus, based on these findings, it can be inferred that self-protective leadership is among the most effective leadership styles for leaders in start-up businesses. Its ability to drive growth, foster resilience, and facilitate organizational effectiveness positions it as a viable choice for leaders aiming to establish sustainable and successful ventures.

Implications of the Study

The qualitative data obtained from the perspectives of the respondents clearly illustrate that the adoption of self-protective leadership style by leaders in start-up businesses yields positive outcomes for organizational effectiveness, while also highlighting various opportunities and challenges associated with this leadership approach. This underscores the significance of self-protective leadership dimensions, including self-centeredness, conflict management, status-consciousness, face-saving, and procedural management, in ensuring business effectiveness within start-up ventures.

From the insights gathered, it becomes apparent that employing self-protective leadership enables leaders to safeguard their businesses and enhance organizational effectiveness. However, alongside these opportunities, there are also notable challenges. For instance, the demands of self-protective leadership can be overwhelming for managers, leading to feelings of exhaustion. Additionally, this leadership style may contribute to higher staff turnover rates within the organization.

An important takeaway from the findings is that, despite the mixed impacts of self-protective leadership on organizational effectiveness, it is evident that this leadership style significantly contributes to positive outcomes within start-up businesses. While acknowledging its potential drawbacks, the overall consensus among respondents is that self-protective leadership fosters effectiveness and success in start-up ventures.

In conclusion, the lessons derived from the data emphasize the importance of understanding the nuanced effects of self-protective leadership on start-up businesses. By recognizing both its strengths and weaknesses, leaders can leverage this leadership style to navigate challenges effectively and drive organizational success in the dynamic landscape of start-up entrepreneurship.

References

Beckman, C. M., Haunschild, P. R., & Phillips, D. J. (2004). Friends or Strangers? Firm-Specific Uncertainty, Market Uncertainty, and Network Partner Selection. *Organization Science, 15*(3), 259–275.

Belderbos, R., Tong, T. W., & Wu, S. (2019). Multinational Investment and the Value of Growth Options: Alignment of Incremental Strategy to Environmental Uncertainty. *Strategic Management Journal, 40*(1), 127–152.

Creswell, J. W. (2014). *Research Design: Qualitative, Quantitative, and Mixed Methods Approaches* (4th ed.). SAGE Publications Ltd.

Creswell, J. W., & Plano Clark, V. L. (2007). *Designing and Conducting Mixed Methods Research.* Sage.

Covin, J. G., & Slevin, D. P. (1989). Strategic Management of Small Firms in Hostile and Benign Environments. *Strategic Management Journal, 10*(1), 75–87.

De Dreu, C. K., & Weingart, L. R. (2003). Task Versus Relationship Conflict, Team Performance, and Team Member Satisfaction: A Meta-Analysis. *Journal of Applied Psychology, 88*(4), 741–749.

De Dreu, C. K. W., & Gelfand, M. J. (Eds.). (2008). *The Psychology of Conflict and Conflict Management in Organizations.* Lawrence Erlbaum Associates.

Eisenhardt, K. M., & Martin, J. A. (2000). Dynamic Capabilities: What Are They? *Strategic Management Journal, 21*(10–11), 1105–1121.

Fayol, H. (1916). *General and Industrial Management*. Pitman.

House, R. J., & Aditya, R. N. (1997). The Social Scientific Study of Leadership: Quo Vadis? *Journal of Management, 23*(3), 409–473.

House, R. J., Hanges, P. J., Javidan, M., Dorfman, P. W., & Gupta, V. (Eds.). (2004). *Culture, Leadership, and Organizations: The GLOBE Study of 62 Societies*. Sage.

Kabasakal, H., Dastmalchian, A., Karacay, G., & Bayraktar, S. (2012). Leadership and Culture in the MENA Region: An Analysis of the GLOBE Project. *Journal of World Business, 47*(4), 519–529.

Leung, K., & Kim, M. S. (2007). Integrating the Complexity of Face in Theories of Negotiation. *Journal of Organizational Behavior, 28*(1), 23–39.

Lipka, R. P., & Brinthaupt, T. M. (1992). *Self-Perspectives Across the Life Span*. SUNY Press.

Mazzei, M. J. (2018). Strategic Entrepreneurship: Content, Process, Context, and Outcomes. *International Entrepreneurship and Management Journal, 14*(3), 657–670.

Mintzberg, H. (1973). *The Nature of Managerial Work*. Harper & Row.

Olaleye, S., Ukpabi, D., & Mogaji, E. (2020). Public vs Private Universities in Nigeria: Market Dynamics Perspective. In E. Mogaji, F. Maringe, & R. E. Hinson (Eds.), *Understanding the Higher Education Market in Africa* (pp. 19–36). Routledge Studies in Marketing.

Tjosvold, D. (2008). The Conflict-Positive Organization: It Depends Upon us. *Journal of Organizational Behavior, 29*(1), 19–28.

Ting-Toomey, S. (1994). Face and Facework: An Introduction. In S. Ting-Toomey (Ed.), *The Challenge of Facework: Cross-Cultural and Interpersonal Issues* (pp. 1–14). State University of New York Press.

Wijbenga, F. H., & Van Witteloostuijn, A. (2007). Entrepreneurial Locus of Control and Competitive Strategies—The Moderating Effect of Environmental Dynamism. *Journal of Economic Psychology, 28*(5), 566–589.

6

Looking Forward: SPL in a New Age of Business

The exploration of self-protective leadership within the marketing communications industry in Ghana and Kenya provides a wealth of insights and actionable recommendations for entrepreneurs and leaders in these markets. These findings hold significant implications for both theory and practice, shedding light on how leadership dynamics influence the survival and effectiveness of start-up businesses (Hofstede, 2001; House et al., 2004).

6.1 Theoretical and Practical Implications

The insights gained from this study are not just academic; they have real-world applications that can guide leaders and entrepreneurs as they navigate the intricate landscape of start-up businesses in Ghana and Kenya. The emphasis on self-protective leadership within these emerging markets offers a unique perspective on how leadership dynamics play out in environments where cultural norms and business practices differ significantly from those in more developed economies (Ang et al., 2007; Thomas, 2006).

D. K. Amoo-Osae, Jr, *Self-Protective Leadership and Organizational Effectiveness*, Palgrave Studies in African Leadership, https://doi.org/10.1007/978-3-031-61308-1_6

One of the most striking practical implications is the need for leaders to develop a deep understanding of the cultural context in which they operate. In Ghana and Kenya, where community ties and relationship-building are central to business success, leaders who are overly self-centered may find themselves isolated, unable to garner the trust and cooperation necessary to lead effectively. This is not just about understanding the surface-level customs but about genuinely appreciating the values that drive people's behavior in these regions (Hofstede, 2001). Leaders who take the time to build relationships, show empathy, and understand the local business environment are more likely to succeed (Trompenaars & Hampden-Turner, 2012). For instance, a leader who prioritizes community engagement and employee well-being over personal gain can create a more cohesive and motivated team, which is crucial for the long-term sustainability of a start-up (Ang et al., 2007).

The theoretical implications of the study extend the conversation about self-protective leadership by providing empirical evidence of its effects in emerging markets. While previous research has established the negative impact of self-centered leadership traits on organizational outcomes, this study goes a step further by contextualizing these findings within the unique challenges of the Ghanaian and Kenyan markets. The integration of behavioral and situational leadership theories within this study offers a nuanced understanding of how self-protective leadership affects organizational effectiveness, particularly in environments where resources are limited, and the business landscape is rapidly evolving (House et al., 2004; Northouse, 2021).

The study also highlights the role of strategic entrepreneurial behavior (SEB) as a potential antidote to the negative effects of self-protective leadership. In environments where innovation and adaptability are critical to survival, SEB can help leaders channel their self-protective tendencies into strategies that benefit the entire organization. For example, a leader who might naturally prioritize their own interests can, through SEB, focus on driving innovation, exploring new markets, and encouraging collaboration among their team (Drucker, 1985). This not only mitigates the potential downsides of self-centeredness but also transforms it into a driver of organizational success (Hisrich et al., 2007).

Moreover, the study's findings suggest that leaders who can blend self-protection with a genuine concern for their employees' well-being are more likely to build resilient organizations. In the context of Ghana and Kenya, where economic and social challenges can be significant, such an approach is not just beneficial but essential (Trompenaars & Hampden-Turner, 2012). Leaders who understand that their success is tied to the success of their team will invest in their employees' growth, foster a collaborative work environment, and build a company culture that values both individual and collective achievements (Northouse, 2021).

In summary, the implications of this study are multifaceted. They provide a roadmap for leaders looking to navigate the complexities of the Ghanaian and Kenyan markets while offering theoretical insights that can inform future research in leadership studies. The key takeaway is that leadership in these contexts requires a delicate balance between self-protection and a genuine concern for others—a balance that, when achieved, can lead to significant organizational success.

6.2 Managerial Implications

The managerial implications outlined in this study offer leaders a comprehensive guide to enhance their leadership practices and improve organizational outcomes. Understanding and addressing the negative aspects of self-centeredness, conflict induction, and procedural rigidity is critical. Leaders who fail to consider their team's input can inadvertently stifle creativity and motivation. Developing self-awareness and emotional intelligence becomes essential in this context, allowing leaders to recognize how their behaviors influence team dynamics and make necessary adjustments to foster a more positive and collaborative environment (Goleman, 1995; Mayer et al., 2008).

Incorporating strategic entrepreneurial behavior (SEB) is equally vital for driving innovation and ensuring long-term success. SEB involves not only encouraging creativity but also providing the necessary resources and opportunities for professional growth. For instance, a start-up might launch a new digital marketing platform, not just as a reactive measure to competition but as a proactive strategy to capture emerging market opportunities. By cultivating an innovative mindset and investing in continuous learning, leaders can position their organizations to stay ahead of the curve and remain competitive in a rapidly changing industry (Drucker, 1985; Hisrich et al., 2007).

Moreover, fostering a culture of open feedback and transparent communication is crucial for building trust and ensuring that the organization remains adaptable. Leaders should actively create avenues where employees feel empowered to share their ideas and concerns. This can be achieved through regular team meetings, anonymous suggestion boxes, or digital platforms that encourage open dialogue. By doing so, leaders not only gain valuable insights into potential issues before they escalate but also reinforce a culture where every team member feels valued and heard (Edmondson, 1999).

In addition to these strategies, leaders should also focus on creating a resilient organizational culture. This involves developing robust support systems that help teams navigate challenges effectively. For instance, offering stress management workshops, mentoring programs, and access to mental health resources can significantly enhance team resilience. When employees are equipped to handle adversity, they are more likely to maintain high levels of productivity and contribute positively to the organization, even in times of crisis (Trompenaars & Hampden-Turner, 2012; Northouse, 2021).

Another key consideration is the importance of ethical leadership. Leaders must consistently demonstrate integrity and accountability in their actions. When leaders take responsibility for their decisions and are transparent about their thought processes, they set a standard for the rest of the organization. This ethical approach fosters a culture of trust, where employees are more likely to follow suit, leading to a more cohesive and ethically grounded organization (Treviño & Nelson, 2021; Baluch & Küpers, 2018).

Finally, it is essential for leaders to continuously align their strategic goals with the evolving needs of the market. This requires staying informed about industry trends, being open to change, and constantly re-evaluating the organization's direction. Leaders who are adaptable and forward-thinking are better positioned to steer their organizations through uncertainty, ensuring not only survival but also growth and success in the long term (D'Aveni, 1994).

By integrating these managerial strategies—ranging from emotional intelligence and innovation to open communication, resilience, ethical leadership, and strategic adaptability—leaders can create a robust framework for leading their organizations effectively in today's dynamic business environment. These approaches are not just recommendations; they are actionable insights that can transform leadership practices and drive organizational success.

6.3 Recommendations for Start-Up Business Leaders

Based on the insights gained from the study, several actionable recommendations emerge for leaders of start-up businesses, particularly within the dynamic and culturally rich contexts of Ghana and Kenya. These recommendations are designed to help leaders navigate the unique challenges of these markets while fostering sustainable organizational growth and success.

Cultivating Self-Awareness:

The journey of leadership begins with self-awareness. Leaders must be acutely aware of how their emotions, decisions, and actions affect their teams. This self-awareness is not a one-time achievement but an ongoing process. Engaging in reflective practices, such as journaling or seeking feedback from trusted colleagues, can be invaluable (Goleman, 1995; Mayer et al., 2008). These practices enable leaders to step back, assess their behavior, and make necessary adjustments to their leadership style. For instance, a leader who regularly reflects on their interactions with employees might identify patterns of behavior that need modification, such as a tendency to dominate conversations or overlook team input. By addressing these issues, leaders can create a more inclusive and supportive environment.

Building and Maintaining Credibility:

Credibility is the cornerstone of effective leadership. It is built over time through consistent actions that demonstrate integrity, accountability, and transparency (Treviño & Nelson, 2021). Leaders who take responsibility for their actions, especially when things go wrong, build trust within their organization. For example, admitting a strategic mistake and outlining clear steps to rectify it not only shows accountability but also sets a powerful example for the rest of the organization. This approach fosters a culture of trust, where employees feel confident in their leadership and are more likely to follow suit in taking responsibility for their own actions.

Embracing Flexibility in Leadership:

In the fast-paced and often unpredictable environment of start-up businesses, flexibility is a crucial trait for leaders. While established protocols and processes provide a necessary structure, there are times when swift, decisive action is required to navigate crises effectively (Northouse, 2021). Leaders who are able to adapt and respond to changing circumstances demonstrate resilience and resourcefulness. For instance, in a marketing start-up facing an unexpected downturn, bypassing traditional approval processes to implement a rapid-response marketing campaign could be the difference between survival and failure. Flexibility ensures that the organization remains agile, capable of responding to both opportunities and threats in a timely manner.

Fostering a Culture of Innovation:

Innovation is the lifeblood of start-ups, and fostering a culture that encourages creative thinking and risk-taking is essential. Leaders play a pivotal role in creating an environment where new ideas are welcomed and explored (Drucker, 1985; Hisrich et al., 2007). This can be achieved by integrating SEB into the organizational culture, where leaders actively encourage experimentation with new advertising platforms, technologies, or business models. By allocating resources to these experimental initiatives, leaders signal their commitment to innovation and position the organization to stay ahead of the competition. For example, a marketing start-up that regularly tests new digital marketing tools may discover a breakthrough strategy that significantly boosts customer engagement and revenue.

Investing in Emotional Intelligence (EI):

The ability to understand and manage emotions—both one's own and those of others—is a critical skill for effective leadership. Investing in EI training for both leaders and their teams can lead to better decision-making, stronger interpersonal relationships, and a more cohesive work environment. Workshops and seminars on EI can provide leaders with the tools they need to navigate the complex emotional dynamics of the workplace. For example, a leader who is emotionally intelligent is better equipped to manage conflicts, motivate their team, and maintain a positive organizational culture, even in challenging times (Goleman, 1995; Mayer et al., 2008).

Promoting Open and Transparent Communication:

Communication is the backbone of any successful organization. Leaders must prioritize open, honest, and transparent communication with their teams. Regular updates on organizational developments, along with a genuine willingness to listen to employee concerns, help build a foundation of trust and engagement (Edmondson, 1999). Monthly town hall meetings or weekly check-ins can facilitate this dialogue, ensuring that employees feel heard and informed. This transparency not only keeps everyone on the same page but also fosters a sense of ownership and accountability throughout the organization.

Encouraging Feedback and Continuous Improvement:

Leaders who actively seek feedback from their employees demonstrate a commitment to continuous improvement. This feedback can be gathered through various channels, such as anonymous surveys, suggestion boxes, or regular one-on-one meetings. By inviting honest input, leaders can gain valuable insights into how their leadership style and organizational processes are perceived by their team. Acting on this feedback to make informed changes benefits the organization and reinforces the value of employee contributions (Treviño & Nelson, 2021).

Leading by Example in Accountability and Integrity:

Leadership is as much about setting an example as it is about making decisions. Leaders who embody accountability and integrity in their actions inspire their teams to do the same. When a leader takes responsibility for a project's failure and works to rectify the situation, it sets a powerful precedent for the rest of the organization. This behavior fosters a culture where trust and reliability are paramount, and where employees feel confident that their efforts are supported by a strong and principled leadership team (Northouse, 2021).

Encouraging Risk-Taking Among Employees:

Innovation does not happen in isolation—it requires the active participation of the entire organization. Leaders can stimulate creative thinking and innovation by organizing initiatives such as innovation challenges or hackathons. These events encourage employees to think outside the box and propose new ideas or solutions that could benefit the organization. By fostering a culture of innovation, leaders not only drive organizational growth but also create an environment where employees feel empowered to contribute their unique perspectives and skills (Drucker, 1985; Hisrich et al., 2007).

Providing Opportunities for Professional Growth and Development:

Retaining and motivating employees is critical to the long-term success of any start-up. Leaders should prioritize the professional development of their team members by offering training programs, mentorship opportunities, and clear paths for career advancement. For example, providing employees with access to courses on new marketing techniques or digital tools can enhance their skills and contribute to the organization's success (Trompenaars & Hampden-Turner, 2012). This investment in employee growth not only improves individual performance but also strengthens the overall capabilities of the organization.

Setting Clear Goals and Expectations:

Clear, well-defined goals are essential for keeping the team aligned with the organization's objectives. Leaders should regularly review and update these goals to ensure they remain relevant and achievable. This ongoing process helps keep the team focused and motivated, providing a clear roadmap for success (Locke & Latham, 2002). For instance, setting quarterly objectives and conducting regular progress reviews can help the team stay on track and make necessary adjustments to achieve desired outcomes.

Supporting Teams in Developing Resilience:

In the face of challenges and adversity, resilience becomes a key determinant of an organization's success. Leaders should support their teams in building resilience by offering resources such as stress management workshops and access to counseling services. By equipping employees with the tools to handle stress and overcome obstacles, leaders ensure that their teams remain productive and positive, even in difficult times (Trompenaars & Hampden-Turner, 2012; Northouse, 2021).

By embracing these recommendations, start-up leaders can effectively harness the strengths of self-protective leadership while mitigating its potential downsides. This balanced approach will enable them to create a positive, supportive work environment that drives organizational success and fosters long-term growth and sustainability for their business.

6.4 Charting the Future of Business: Benchmarks for New and Emerging Enterprises

In today's interconnected and rapidly changing globalized economy, leadership styles, including self-protective leadership, are increasingly scrutinized. The globalized economy presents a complex landscape characterized by heightened competition, technological advancements, cultural diversity, and interconnected markets. Within this dynamic environment, self-protective leadership's fate is shaped by evolutionary dynamics influenced by numerous factors (Friedman, 2005; Andresen & Burke, 2020).

Adaptability Amidst Global Turbulence

Self-protective leadership, marked by tendencies to safeguard personal or organizational interests, faces unique challenges and opportunities in this globalized economy. Leaders must navigate a landscape fraught with uncertainty, volatility, and rapid technological advancements. The ability to adapt and evolve amidst global turbulence is crucial for leaders practicing self-protection. In an era where disruptive forces such as globalization, digitization, and geopolitical shifts can redefine industry landscapes overnight, leaders must continuously reassess their strategies and behaviors to remain relevant and effective (Northouse, 2021; Hill et al., 2014).

For instance, consider a start-up in Ghana that has traditionally relied heavily on local markets but suddenly faces international competition due to globalization. A self-protective leader might initially resist change, aiming to protect the company's existing market share. However, true adaptability lies in recognizing that change can also present opportunities. By embracing new technologies, exploring global markets, and forming strategic partnerships, a leader can turn potential threats into growth opportunities (Teece, 2007). For example, a Ghanaian marketing communications firm might expand its reach by partnering with international firms, leveraging global networks to enhance its market presence and competitiveness.

In such scenarios, self-protective leaders who are too rigid in their strategies may find themselves outpaced by more adaptive competitors. However, those who are willing to evolve—by integrating global best practices, adopting new technologies, and being open to cross-cultural collaborations—can thrive even in turbulent conditions (Ghemawat, 2011). This adaptability not only preserves the organization's competitive edge but also positions it for long-term success in a rapidly changing global marketplace.

Self-protective leadership in a global context requires a delicate balance: leaders must protect their organizations from external threats while remaining open to new opportunities that global changes bring. This involves staying informed about global trends, understanding the implications of technological advancements, and being agile enough to pivot strategies when necessary. Leaders who master this balance will be better equipped to lead their organizations through the complexities of the globalized economy, ensuring their relevance and success in the future (D'Aveni, 1994).

Cultural Sensitivity and Cross-Border Leadership

Thriving in today's interconnected business world requires leaders to go beyond traditional strategies and embrace the nuances of cultural sensitivity, particularly when leading across borders. Leaders who practice self-protection must understand that while their core leadership style may remain consistent, the application of that style needs to be flexible and adaptable to different cultural contexts (Earley & Ang, 2003).

In cross-border leadership, cultural sensitivity is not just an added skill—it is a necessity. Leaders who can adeptly navigate cultural differences will find themselves better positioned to build trust and foster collaboration with stakeholders from diverse backgrounds. This involves recognizing and respecting varying cultural norms, values, and business practices (Hofstede, 2001). For example, a Kenyan start-up aiming to expand into new African markets must acknowledge that what works in Nairobi might not necessarily succeed in Lagos or Johannesburg. Each market comes with its own set of cultural expectations and business etiquette, which must be carefully considered.

Effective cross-border leadership means engaging in continuous learning about local cultures and integrating that knowledge into everyday business practices. This might involve adjusting communication styles to suit local preferences, modifying marketing strategies to resonate with cultural values, or even altering negotiation tactics to align with local norms. By doing so, leaders not only avoid potential cultural missteps but also demonstrate respect and understanding, which can significantly enhance their credibility and effectiveness (Schneider & Barsoux, 2003).

Moreover, cultural sensitivity helps in conflict resolution and in building long-term relationships, which are crucial for sustained success in foreign markets. For instance, understanding the importance of hierarchical respect in certain cultures can guide a leader's approach to decision-making and employee interaction, fostering a more harmonious and productive work environment (Trompenaars & Hampden-Turner, 2012).

When leaders blend self-protective leadership with cultural sensitivity, they create a powerful combination that not only protects their organization's interests but also opens doors to new opportunities. This approach allows leaders to maintain their strategic focus while being adaptable to the diverse and dynamic global market, ultimately leading to more sustainable growth and success across borders.

In essence, cultural sensitivity is not just a leadership skill—it's a strategic advantage that can significantly impact the success of expanding into new and diverse markets. When leaders respect and integrate cultural differences into their leadership practices, they not only safeguard their organization's reputation but also foster a culture of inclusivity and innovation that drives long-term success (Hofstede, 2001).

Ethical Considerations and Corporate Governance

As the business landscape becomes more globalized and interconnected, the importance of ethical leadership and strong corporate governance cannot be overstated. Leaders are increasingly faced with the challenge of upholding high ethical standards while navigating complex international markets where the consequences of unethical behavior can ripple across borders almost instantly. This makes the role of ethics in leadership not just a matter of compliance but a fundamental aspect of long-term business sustainability (Treviño & Nelson, 2021).

Ethical leadership is the bedrock of corporate governance. It goes beyond merely following laws and regulations; it involves fostering a corporate culture where ethical behavior is encouraged, valued, and ingrained in every business decision. This might include establishing clear ethical guidelines, conducting regular training sessions to reinforce these values, and ensuring that all employees understand the importance of integrity in their daily work. Leaders must also model these behaviors, demonstrating through their actions that ethical considerations are a priority at the highest levels of the organization (Northouse, 2021).

The stakes are high in today's global economy. A lapse in ethical judgment can lead to severe consequences, such as legal penalties, loss of consumer trust, and significant damage to a company's reputation. For instance, a start-up in Kenya that engages in unethical practices could face repercussions that extend far beyond its local market, potentially affecting its ability to secure international partnerships or investment. To mitigate such risks, leaders should prioritize transparency and accountability, ensuring that their corporate governance structures are robust enough to detect and address unethical behavior promptly (D'Aveni, 1994).

Moreover, strong corporate governance mechanisms serve as a critical line of defense against ethical breaches. These mechanisms include not only the establishment of policies and procedures that promote ethical behavior but also the implementation of effective oversight and enforcement measures. Regular audits, independent board oversight, and clear reporting channels for ethical concerns are essential components of a governance framework that can uphold ethical standards in a complex and rapidly changing business environment (Hill et al., 2014; Treviño & Nelson, 2021).

In summary, ethical considerations and corporate governance are not just about protecting the organization from legal or financial fallout; they are about building a foundation of trust with stakeholders, including customers, employees, investors, and the broader community. By prioritizing ethics and governance, leaders can ensure that their organizations are resilient, respected, and positioned for long-term success in the global marketplace.

Strategic Leadership and Innovation

In the age of globalization and competition, strategic leadership is a critical element for navigating business complexities and seizing opportunities. For leaders who lean toward self-protection, adopting a strategic mindset becomes even more crucial. Strategic leadership goes beyond mere decision-making; it involves a visionary approach where leaders must anticipate future trends, identify potential challenges, and craft strategies that align with both short-term objectives and long-term goals. The ability to foresee and adapt to global shifts in markets, technology, and consumer behavior is what separates thriving organizations from those that merely survive (Northouse, 2021; Teece, 2007).

Innovation serves as the cornerstone of strategic leadership, particularly in a world where digital transformation and technological advancements continuously reshape industries. Leaders need to embrace innovation not only as a driver of efficiency but as a core component of their competitive strategy. A start-up in Kenya, for example, might gain a significant edge by adopting advanced marketing technologies such as AI-driven analytics or social media automation tools. These innovations can open new channels for customer engagement, drive sales, and enhance brand visibility on a global scale (Deloitte Insights, 2020).

To sustain innovation, leaders must cultivate a culture that encourages creativity, experimentation, and collaboration within their teams. This involves creating an environment where employees feel empowered to propose new ideas and take calculated risks without the fear of failure. Leaders should also emphasize the importance of continuous learning and adaptation, recognizing that flexibility in strategy and operations is essential in a rapidly changing world. Investing in training programs, fostering interdisciplinary teams, and maintaining an open dialogue about emerging trends can help an organization stay ahead of the curve (Hill et al., 2014; Hamel, 2000).

Moreover, strategic leadership requires balancing the internal strengths of the organization with the external demands of the global market. This might involve rethinking traditional business models, exploring new revenue streams, or entering partnerships that enhance the organization's capabilities. For instance, forming strategic alliances with international firms could provide a Kenyan start-up with access to new technologies, markets, and expertise, thereby amplifying its global footprint (Ghemawat, 2011).

Thus by integrating strategic leadership with a strong commitment to innovation, leaders can navigate the complexities of the global economy more effectively. This approach not only mitigates the inherent risks of a self-protective leadership style but also transforms these risks into opportunities for growth, ensuring that the organization remains resilient, competitive, and poised for long-term success (Friedman, 2005; D'Aveni, 1994).

6.5 Conclusion

The exploration of self-protective leadership in Ghana and Kenya's marketing communications industry unveils a nuanced understanding of how leadership styles must evolve in a globalized world. As markets become more interconnected, the demands on leaders intensify, requiring them to not only protect their organizations but also to embrace a broader, more adaptive approach.

Self-protective leadership, while essential in shielding organizations from risks, must be balanced with cultural sensitivity, ethical governance, and a strategic vision that prioritizes innovation and collaboration. In today's diverse and fast-paced business environment, leaders who can navigate cultural differences with empathy and respect will find themselves better positioned to build strong, lasting relationships. This is not just about avoiding missteps; it's about creating a leadership style that resonates across borders, fostering trust and cooperation in a variety of cultural contexts.

Ethical leadership has never been more crucial. In a world where corporate scandals can erupt and spread globally within moments, maintaining integrity and transparency is paramount. Leaders must go beyond mere compliance, embedding ethical practices into the very fabric of their organizations. This commitment to doing the right thing builds a foundation of trust that not only protects the organization but also strengthens its reputation, paving the way for long-term success.

Strategic leadership is the driving force behind innovation and adaptability. Leaders must be forward-thinking, constantly scanning the horizon for emerging trends and potential disruptions. By fostering a culture of innovation, they encourage their teams to think creatively and embrace change, turning potential threats into opportunities for growth. This is particularly important in a globalized economy, where the ability to pivot quickly can be the difference between success and failure.

The future of self-protective leadership lies invariably in its capacity to evolve. Leaders who can balance protection with a commitment to innovation, ethical practices, and cultural sensitivity will not only safeguard their organizations but will also propel them to new heights in an increasingly interconnected world. This balanced approach is key to ensuring the long-term sustainability and success of any organization navigating the complexities of the global economy.

References

Andresen, M., & Burke, R. J. (2020). *Handbook of Research on Expatriates.* Edward Elgar Publishing.

Ang, S., Van Dyne, L., & Koh, C. (2007). Cultural Intelligence: Its Measurement and Effects on Cultural Judgment and Decision Making, Cultural

Adaptation and Task Performance. *Management and Organization Review, 3*(3), 335–371.
Baluch, A. M., & Küpers, W. (2018). Ethical Leadership in Practice: A Phenomenological Perspective. *Journal of Business Ethics, 154*(3), 513–527.
D'Aveni, R. A. (1994). *Hypercompetition: Managing the Dynamics of Strategic Maneuvering*. Free Press.
Deloitte Insights. (2020). *Tech Trends 2020: The Fusion of Business and Technology*. Deloitte University Press.
Drucker, P. F. (1985). *Innovation and Entrepreneurship: Practice and Principles.* Harper & Row.
Earley, P. C., & Ang, S. (2003). *Cultural Intelligence: Individual Interactions Across Cultures.* Stanford University Press.
Edmondson, A. (1999). Psychological Safety and Learning Behavior in Work Teams. *Administrative Science Quarterly, 44*(2), 350–383.
Friedman, T. L. (2005). *The World Is Flat: A Brief History of the Twenty-First Century*. Farrar, Straus, and Giroux.
Ghemawat, P. (2011). *World 3.0: Global Prosperity and How to Achieve It.* Harvard Business Review Press.
Goleman, D. (1995). *Emotional Intelligence: Why It Can Matter More Than IQ*. Bantam Books.
Hamel, G. (2000). *Leading the Revolution.* Harvard Business School Press.
Hill, C. W. L., Jones, G. R., & Schilling, M. A. (2014). *Strategic Management. Theory: An Integrated Approach*. Cengage Learning.
Hisrich, R. D., Peters, M. P., & Shepherd, D. A. (2007). *Entrepreneurship* (7th ed.). McGraw-Hill.
Hofstede, G. (2001). *Culture's Consequences: Comparing Values, Behaviors, Institutions, and Organizations Across Nations*. Sage Publications.
House, R. J., Hanges, P. J., Javidan, M., Dorfman, P. W., & Gupta, V. (Eds.). (2004). *Culture, Leadership, and Organizations: The GLOBE Study of 62 Societies*. Sage Publications.
Locke, E. A., & Latham, G. P. (2002). Building a Practically Useful Theory of Goal Setting and Task Motivation: A 35-year Odyssey. *American Psychologist, 57*(9), 705–717.
Mayer, J. D., Salovey, P., & Caruso, D. R. (2008). Emotional Intelligence: New Ability or Eclectic Traits? *American Psychologist, 63*(6), 503–517.
Northouse, P. G. (2021). *Leadership: Theory and Practice* (9th ed.). Sage Publications.
Schneider, S. C., & Barsoux, J. L. (2003). *Managing Across Cultures*. Pearson Education.

Teece, D. J. (2007). Explicating Dynamic Capabilities: The Nature and Microfoundations of (sustainable) Enterprise Performance. *Strategic Management Journal, 28*(13), 1319–1350.

Treviño, L. K., & Nelson, K. A. (2021). *Managing Business Ethics: Straight Talk About How to Do It Right* (8th ed.). Wiley.

Trompenaars, F., & Hampden-Turner, C. (2012). *Riding the Waves of Culture: Understanding Diversity in Global Business*. Nicholas Brealey Publishing.

Appendices

Appendix 1: Statement on Research Methodology

This study employed a mixed-method approach, integrating both quantitative and qualitative data collection and analysis to provide a comprehensive understanding of the self-protective leadership style's impact on start-up businesses in the marketing communication sector.

Quantitative Methodology

For the quantitative aspect, a structured questionnaire was developed to gather data from start-up businesses in Ghana and Kenya. The target sample size was 174 participants from Ghana and 240 from Kenya. The questionnaire included sections on demographics and key constructs such as self-centeredness, status-consciousness, conflict induction, face-saving, and procedural adherence, all attributes of self-protective leadership. Participants rated these items using a Likert scale from 1 (strongly disagree) to 5 (strongly agree).

Data collection was facilitated by trained research assistants who distributed the questionnaires while adhering to COVID-19 protocols.

D. K. Amoo-Osae, Jr, *Self-Protective Leadership and Organizational Effectiveness*, Palgrave Studies in African Leadership, https://doi.org/10.1007/978-3-031-61308-1

Participants were given four weeks to complete and return the questionnaires, with reminders sent to ensure a high response rate. The final sample comprised 233 responses from Kenya (77% retrieval rate) and 129 responses from Ghana (88% retrieval rate).

The quantitative data were screened for completeness and cleaned of any inconsistencies. Outlier cases were evaluated using Mahalanobis distance and Cook's D tests, ensuring the integrity of the dataset. The cleaned data were analyzed using several statistical tools:

- Descriptive Statistics: To summarize the basic features of the data, providing simple summaries about the sample and measures.
- Reliability Analysis: Cronbach's alpha was used to assess the internal consistency of the scales, ensuring the reliability of the constructs.
- Exploratory Factor Analysis (EFA): This was used to identify the underlying relationships between measured variables. The factor loading criteria of 0.50 and above were applied to confirm the construct validity.
- Confirmatory Factor Analysis (CFA): Conducted using Structural Equation Modeling (SEM) to validate the factor structure identified in EFA and to test the fit of the measurement model.
- Regression Analysis: Multiple regression analysis was employed to examine the relationships between self-protective leadership dimensions and start-up business survival and effectiveness.
- Moderation Analysis: Using interaction terms in regression models to assess the moderating effect of strategic entrepreneurial behavior on the relationship between self-protective leadership and business outcomes.

Qualitative Methodology

The qualitative component utilized a case study approach to gain deeper insights into the practical applications of self-protective leadership. Eight start-up entrepreneurs from the marketing communication sector were selected through purposive sampling. This method ensured that participants had relevant experience and expertise to provide valuable information.

In-depth interviews were conducted, either face-to-face, over the phone, or via the internet, to accommodate participants' preferences and enhance response rates. The interviews were guided by a semi-structured interview guide, which allowed for flexibility in exploring specific topics while ensuring consistency across interviews. The guide included open-ended questions designed to elicit detailed responses about the impact of self-protective leadership on their businesses.

The qualitative data were transcribed and analyzed using content analysis methods. The analytical process included:

- Coding: Transcripts were coded to identify key themes and patterns related to self-protective leadership and its impact.
- Thematic Analysis: Themes were developed from the codes to capture the essence of the participants' experiences and perspectives.
- Cross-Case Analysis: Comparing and contrasting themes across different cases to identify commonalities and differences in the implementation and outcomes of self-protective leadership.

Appendix 2: Common Method Bias

Component	Initial eigenvalues			Extraction sums of squared loadings		
	Total	% of variance	Cumulative %	Total	% of variance	Cumulative %
1	20.492	24.109	24.109	20.492	24.109	24.109
2	8.436	9.925	34.033			
3	3.316	3.901	37.935			
4	3.111	3.660	41.594			
5	2.786	3.278	44.872			
6	2.471	2.907	47.779			
7	2.313	2.722	50.501			
8	2.156	2.537	53.038			
9	1.820	2.141	55.179			
10	1.610	1.894	57.073			
11	1.567	1.844	58.916			
12	1.412	1.662	60.578			
13	1.354	1.593	62.171			
14	1.292	1.520	63.691			
15	1.211	1.424	65.115			
16	1.082	1.273	66.388			
17	1.001	1.178	67.566			
18	0.956	1.125	68.690			
19	0.944	1.110	69.800			
20	0.915	1.077	70.877			
21	0.874	1.028	71.906			
22	0.838	0.985	72.891			
23	0.793	0.933	73.824			
24	0.772	0.908	74.733			
25	0.755	0.888	75.620			
26	0.737	0.867	76.488			
27	0.691	0.812	77.300			
28	0.683	0.803	78.103			

(continued)

(continued)

Component	Initial eigenvalues			Extraction sums of squared loadings		
	Total	% of variance	Cumulative %	Total	% of variance	Cumulative %
29	0.664	0.781	78.884			
30	0.660	0.777	79.661			
31	0.654	0.769	80.430			
32	0.614	0.722	81.152			
33	0.607	0.714	81.866			

Appendix 3: Normality Diagrams

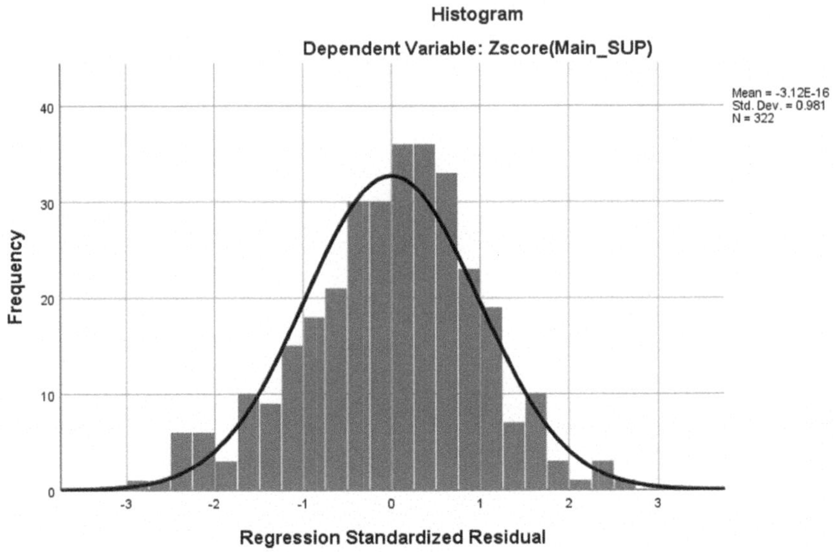

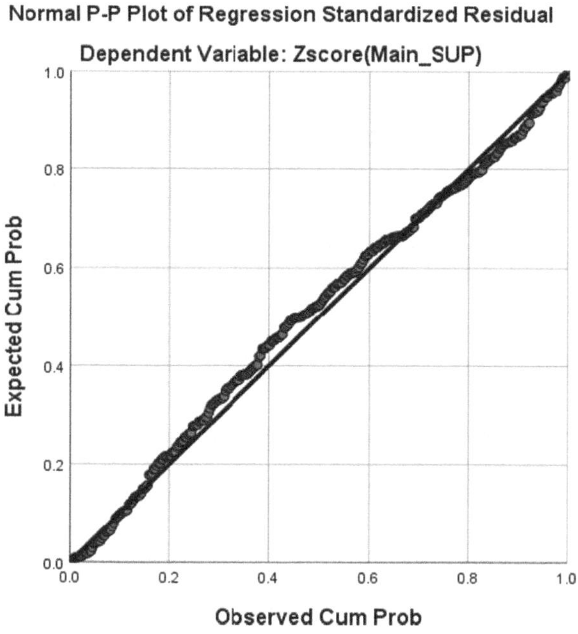

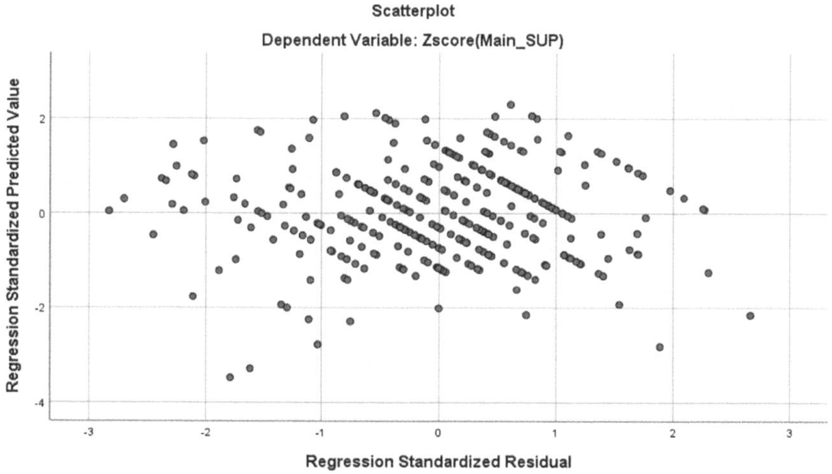

Appendix 4: Presentation of Variables, Kenya

	N	Min	Max	Mean	Std. Deviation	Skewness		Kurtosis	
	Statistic	Statistic	Statistic	Statistic	Statistic	Statistic	Std. Error	Statistic	Std. Error
SCL1	128	1.00	5.00	3.953	0.955	−1.285	0.214	1.743	0.425
SCL2	128	1.00	5.00	3.750	1.065	−1.232	0.214	0.983	0.425
SCL3	128	2.00	5.00	3.914	0.870	−0.780	0.214	0.199	0.425
SCL4	128	1.00	5.00	3.898	0.912	−0.998	0.214	0.957	0.425
SCL5	128	1.00	5.00	3.891	0.990	−1.162	0.214	1.323	0.425
FSL1	128	1.00	5.00	4.164	0.954	−1.608	0.214	3.017	0.425
FSL2	128	1.00	5.00	4.000	0.988	−1.094	0.214	1.119	0.425
FSL3	128	1.00	5.00	3.945	1.014	−1.178	0.214	1.228	0.425
PL1	128	1.00	5.00	4.039	1.007	−0.972	0.214	0.324	0.425
PL2	128	2.00	5.00	4.078	0.993	−0.845	0.214	−0.340	0.425
PL3	128	1.00	5.00	4.039	1.045	−1.087	0.214	0.535	0.425
SL1	128	1.00	5.00	2.211	1.141	0.707	0.214	−0.480	0.425
SL2	128	1.00	5.00	2.094	1.053	0.796	0.214	−0.208	0.425
SL3	128	1.00	5.00	2.094	1.075	0.930	0.214	0.199	0.425
SL4	128	1.00	5.00	2.094	1.061	0.816	0.214	−0.210	0.425
SL5	128	1.00	5.00	2.078	1.047	0.845	0.214	0.067	0.425
CI1	128	1.00	5.00	1.961	1.060	0.964	0.214	0.037	0.425
CI2	128	1.00	5.00	1.789	0.953	1.268	0.214	1.271	0.425
CI3	128	1.00	5.00	1.914	1.004	0.980	0.214	0.322	0.425
CI4	128	1.00	5.00	1.844	1.031	1.240	0.214	1.116	0.425
CI6	128	1.00	5.00	1.836	0.986	1.137	0.214	0.734	0.425
SEB1	128	1.00	5.00	3.383	0.948	0.175	0.214	−0.121	0.425
SEB2	128	1.00	5.00	3.273	0.830	0.205	0.214	0.360	0.425
SEB3	128	1.00	5.00	3.219	0.860	−0.138	0.214	0.710	0.425
SEB4	128	1.00	5.00	3.266	0.900	−0.027	0.214	0.825	0.425

(continued)

(continued)

	N	Min	Max	Mean	Std. Deviation	Skewness		Kurtosis	
	Statistic	Statistic	Statistic	Statistic	Statistic	Statistic	Std. Error	Statistic	Std. Error
OE1	128	1.00	5.00	2.938	0.962	0.072	0.214	−0.437	0.425
OE2	128	1.00	5.00	2.961	0.991	0.128	0.214	−0.454	0.425
OE3	128	2.00	5.00	4.023	0.768	−0.993	0.214	1.387	0.425
MD1	128	1.00	5.00	3.625	0.878	−0.389	0.214	0.162	0.425
MD2	128	1.00	5.00	3.422	0.848	−0.382	0.214	0.409	0.425
MD3	128	1.00	5.00	3.430	0.781	−0.116	0.214	0.637	0.425
MD4	128	1.00	5.00	3.430	0.810	0.051	0.214	0.002	0.425
MD5	128	1.00	5.00	3.469	0.783	−0.145	0.214	0.121	0.425
MD6	128	1.00	5.00	3.383	0.814	−0.014	0.214	0.372	0.425
MD7	128	1.00	5.00	3.406	0.818	−0.176	0.214	0.292	0.425
TD1	128	1.00	5.00	3.375	0.687	−0.647	0.214	1.078	0.425
TD2	128	1.00	5.00	3.164	0.840	−0.481	0.214	0.611	0.425
TD3	128	1.00	5.00	3.242	0.761	−0.658	0.214	0.324	0.425
MU1	128	1.00	5.00	2.078	1.084	0.446	0.214	−1.049	0.425
MU2	128	1.00	5.00	2.320	1.216	0.268	0.214	−1.055	0.425
MU3	128	1.00	5.00	4.219	0.878	−1.225	0.214	1.406	0.425
ED1	128	1.00	5.00	4.102	0.895	−1.073	0.214	0.994	0.425
ED2	128	1.00	5.00	4.047	0.971	−1.039	0.214	0.687	0.425
ED3	128	1.00	5.00	3.820	0.943	−0.491	0.214	−0.333	0.425
ED4	128	1.00	5.00	3.719	0.930	−0.660	0.214	0.416	0.425
ED5	128	1.00	5.00	3.617	0.948	−0.400	0.214	−0.006	0.425

Note SCL = Status Conscious, FSL = Face-Saving, PL = Procedural, SL = Self-Centered, CI = Conflict Inducer, SEB = Strategic Entrepreneurial Behavior, OE = Organizational Effectiveness and MD = Market Dynamism, TD = Technological Dynamism, MU = Market Uncertainty and ED = Environmental Dynamism

Appendix 5: Presentation of Variables, Ghana

	N	Min	Max	Mean	Std. Deviation	Skewness		Kurtosis	
	Statistic	Statistic	Statistic	Statistic	Statistic	Statistic	Std. Error	Statistic	Std. Error
SCL1	233	1.00	5.00	3.970	0.893	−0.957	0.159	1.084	0.316
SCL2	233	1.00	5.00	3.736	1.037	−0.520	0.159	−0.416	0.316
SCL3	233	1.00	5.00	4.038	0.802	−0.620	0.159	0.569	0.316
SCL4	233	1.00	5.00	4.204	0.796	−1.153	0.159	2.237	0.316
SCL5	233	1.00	5.00	4.132	0.765	−0.864	0.159	1.495	0.316
FSL1	233	1.00	5.00	4.166	0.833	−0.946	0.159	1.199	0.316
FSL2	233	1.00	5.00	4.051	0.794	−0.661	0.159	0.734	0.316
FSL3	233	1.00	5.00	3.613	1.074	−0.766	0.159	0.142	0.316
PL1	233	1.00	5.00	4.055	0.785	−0.792	0.159	1.183	0.316
PL2	233	1.00	5.00	3.689	0.939	−0.279	0.159	−0.373	0.316
PL3	233	1.00	5.00	3.966	0.816	−0.604	0.159	0.531	0.316
SL1	233	1.00	5.00	3.123	1.280	−0.356	0.159	−1.070	0.316
SL2	233	1.00	5.00	3.000	1.169	−0.388	0.159	−0.769	0.316
SL3	233	1.00	5.00	3.153	1.159	−0.601	0.159	−0.707	0.316
SL4	233	1.00	5.00	3.179	1.203	−0.423	0.159	−0.761	0.316
SL5	233	1.00	5.00	3.187	1.180	−0.479	0.159	−0.745	0.316
CI1	233	1.00	5.00	2.604	1.285	0.053	0.159	−1.436	0.316
CI2	233	1.00	5.00	2.736	1.257	0.158	0.159	−1.044	0.316
CI3	233	1.00	5.00	2.617	1.290	0.166	0.159	−1.275	0.316
CI4	233	1.00	5.00	2.562	1.261	0.279	0.159	−1.012	0.316
CI5	233	1.00	5.00	2.226	1.200	0.649	0.159	−0.658	0.316
SEB1	233	1.00	5.00	3.919	0.788	−0.805	0.159	1.496	0.316
SEB2	233	1.00	5.00	3.438	0.938	−0.008	0.159	−0.480	0.316
SEB3	233	1.00	5.00	3.694	0.929	−0.740	0.159	0.632	0.316
SEB4	233	1.00	5.00	3.860	0.858	−0.421	0.159	−0.212	0.316
OE1	233	1.00	5.00	3.983	0.722	−0.800	0.159	1.951	0.316

(continued)

(continued)

	N	Min	Max	Mean	Std. Deviation	Skewness		Kurtosis	
	Statistic	Statistic	Statistic	Statistic	Statistic	Statistic	Std. Error	Statistic	Std. Error
OE2	233	1.00	5.00	3.919	0.846	−0.059	0.159	−0.952	0.316
OE3	233	2.00	5.00	3.945	0.785	−0.597	0.159	0.231	0.316
MD1	233	1.00	5.00	4.030	0.759	−0.937	0.159	1.898	0.316
MD2	233	1.00	5.00	3.515	0.859	−0.475	0.159	0.564	0.316
MD3	233	1.00	5.00	3.851	0.847	−0.861	0.159	0.801	0.316
MD4	233	2.00	5.00	3.800	0.831	−0.016	0.159	−0.850	0.316
MD5	233	1.00	5.00	3.106	1.181	−0.239	0.159	−0.907	0.316
MD6	233	1.00	5.00	3.123	1.124	−0.227	0.159	−0.638	0.316
MD7	233	1.00	5.00	3.345	1.052	−0.683	0.159	−0.058	0.316
TD1	233	1.00	5.00	4.149	0.762	−0.901	0.159	1.621	0.316
TD2	233	1.00	5.00	3.936	0.827	−0.429	0.159	0.098	0.316
TD3	233	1.00	5.00	3.970	0.819	−0.416	0.159	−0.169	0.316
MU1	233	1.00	5.00	4.047	0.675	−0.983	0.159	2.777	0.316
MU2	233	1.00	5.00	3.689	0.868	−0.024	0.159	−0.582	0.316
MU3	233	1.00	5.00	3.409	1.095	−0.453	0.159	−0.609	0.316
ED1	233	1.00	5.00	3.681	0.981	−1.270	0.159	1.541	0.316
ED2	233	1.00	5.00	3.426	0.885	−0.424	0.159	0.494	0.316
ED3	233	1.00	5.00	3.609	0.842	−0.714	0.159	0.176	0.316
ED4	233	1.00	5.00	3.353	1.012	−0.754	0.159	0.296	0.316
ED5	233	1.00	5.00	3.668	0.863	−0.632	0.159	0.519	0.316

Note SCL = Status Conscious, FSL = Face-Saving, PL = Procedural, SL = Self-Centered, CI = Conflict Inducer, SEB = Strategic Entrepreneurial Behavior, OE = Organizational Effectiveness and MD = Market Dynamism, TD = Technological Dynamism, MU = Market Uncertainty and ED = Environmental Dynamism

Appendix 6: Demographic Characteristics of Research Sample

	Residence			
	Ghana sample		Kenya sample	
Variable/characteristics	Frequency	Percent %	Frequency	Percent %
Gender				
Male	62	48.1	176	74.9
Female	67	51.9	57	24.3
Age				
18–30 years	80	62.0	83	35.6
31–40 years	40	31.0	102	43.8
41–50 years	7	5.4	24	10.3
51–60 years	1	0.8	21	9
61 years and above	1	0.8	3	1.3
Education				
Diploma	3	2.3	108	46.3
Bachelors	108	83.7	69	29.6
Masters	16	12.4	2	0.9
PhD/DBA	1	0.8	2	0.9
Others	1	0.8	52	22.3
Number of years worked				
Less than 2 years	66	51.2	54	23.2
2–3 years	53	41.1	67	28.7
4 years and above	10	7.7	112	48.1
Years of operation				
Below 1 year	16	12.4	5	2.1
1–2 years	13	10.1	16	6.9
2–3 years	32	24.8	47	20.2
3–4 years	23	17.8	34	14.6
4–5 years	45	34.9	131	56.2

Appendix 7: Exploratory Factor Analysis (Main Variables), Kenya

Items	Component						
	1	2	3	4	5	6	7
SCL1	−0.181	**0.690**	−0.348	0.201	0.157	0.150	0.138
SCL2	−0.374	**0.719**	−0.210	0.002	0.212	0.039	0.209
SCL3	−0.323	**0.698**	−0.317	0.150	0.114	0.168	0.211
SCL4	−0.229	**0.828**	−0.172	0.174	0.133	0.161	0.177
SCL5	−0.372	**0.750**	−0.260	0.112	0.264	0.095	0.071
FSL1	−0.092	0.154	−0.349	0.219	0.080	0.096	**0.795**
FSL2	−0.316	0.429	−0.176	0.078	0.381	0.211	**0.601**
FSL3	−0.321	0.460	−0.173	0.025	0.328	0.226	**0.605**
PL1	−0.318	0.403	−0.285	0.049	**0.739**	0.178	0.105
PL2	−0.225	0.378	−0.285	0.110	**0.742**	0.220	0.192
PL3	−0.208	0.340	−0.312	0.103	**0.728**	0.269	0.135
SCCL1	**0.792**	−0.299	0.287	−0.030	−0.106	−0.148	−0.177
SCCL2	**0.826**	−0.288	0.250	−0.044	−0.248	−0.097	−0.088
SCCL3	**0.846**	−0.290	0.235	0.010	−0.174	−0.090	−0.144
SCCL4	**0.842**	−0.265	0.240	−0.095	−0.231	−0.083	0.020
SCCL5	**0.819**	−0.293	0.284	−0.011	−0.037	−0.130	−0.190
CI1	0.330	−0.255	**0.794**	−0.162	−0.173	−0.176	−0.130
CI2	0.415	−0.328	**0.745**	−0.092	−0.226	−0.162	−0.106
CI3	0.413	−0.353	**0.736**	−0.112	−0.230	−0.078	−0.151
CI4	0.351	−0.273	**0.783**	−0.163	−0.220	−0.216	−0.149
CI5	0.349	−0.250	**0.783**	−0.171	−0.218	−0.195	−0.120
CI6	0.353	−0.299	**0.762**	−0.155	−0.148	−0.204	−0.207
OE1	−0.034	0.135	−0.154	0.253	0.078	**0.873**	0.173
OE2	−0.112	0.147	−0.218	0.224	0.197	**0.868**	0.084
OE3	−0.185	0.177	−0.182	0.225	0.179	**0.869**	0.146
SEB1	−0.078	0.094	−0.045	**0.881**	0.023	0.036	0.030

(continued)

(continued)

Items	Component						
	1	2	3	4	5	6	7
SEB2	−0.043	0.116	−0.056	**0.876**	0.164	0.142	0.067
SEB3	−0.085	0.029	−0.095	**0.887**	−0.017	0.129	0.174
SEB4	−0.021	−0.009	−0.171	**0.862**	0.156	0.076	0.100
Eigen values	24.036	5.161	2.500	2.216	1.717	1.429	1.237
Percentage of variance explained	18.331	17.495	14.786	11.582	9.534	9.267	6.041
Cumulative % of variance explained	18.331	35.826	50.612	62.194	71.727	80.995	87.036
KMO and Bartlett's test of sphericity	KMO = 0.909, Bartlett's test of sphericity χ^2 (946) = 8988.139, $p < 0.001$						

Note SCL = Self-Centered Leadership, FSL = Face-Saving Leadership, PL = Procedural Leadership, SCCL = Status-Conscious Leadership, CI = Conflict Inducer Leadership, OE = Organizational Effectiveness, SEB = Strategic Entrepreneurial Behavior

Appendix 8: Exploratory Factor Analysis (Control Variables), Kenya

Items	Component			
	1	2	3	4
MD1	**0.740**	0.232	0.135	0.103
MD2	**0.761**	0.155	0.276	0.201
MD3	**0.790**	0.203	0.064	0.228
MD4	**0.852**	0.173	0.213	0.163
MD5	**0.901**	0.203	0.131	0.126
MD6	**0.830**	0.195	0.156	0.104
MD7	**0.884**	0.141	0.113	0.119
TD1	0.383	0.221	0.284	**0.626**
TD2	0.251	0.039	0.108	**0.809**
TD3	0.094	0.186	0.168	**0.848**
MU1	0.235	0.325	**0.848**	0.159
MU2	0.215	0.323	**0.875**	0.214
MU3	0.241	0.286	**0.847**	0.197
ED1	0.283	**0.813**	0.252	0.133
ED2	0.309	**0.828**	0.240	0.126
ED3	0.210	**0.790**	0.304	0.089
ED4	0.183	**0.901**	0.169	0.104
ED5	0.128	**0.860**	0.135	0.117
Eigen values	9.245	2.525	1.562	1.116
Percentage of variance explained	30.035	23.043	15.456	11.731
Cumulative % of variance explained	30.035	53.078	68.535	80.266
KMO and Bartlett's test of sphericity	KMO = 0.861, Bartlett's test of sphericity χ^2 (153) = 2384.708, $p < 0.001$			

Note MD = Market Dynamism, TD = Technological Dynamism, MU = Market Uncertainty, ED = Environmental Dynamism

Appendix 9: Exploratory Factor Analysis (Main Variables), Ghana

Items	Component						
	1	2	3	4	5	6	7
SCL1	−0.077	−0.100	−0.012	0.213	−0.080	**0.706**	0.115
SCL2	−0.185	0.041	0.146	0.012	0.098	**0.770**	0.072
SCL3	−0.066	−0.257	0.042	0.142	0.226	**0.510**	0.194
SCL5	−0.064	0.037	0.045	−0.001	0.036	**0.675**	0.125
FSL1	−0.076	−0.213	0.068	0.060	−0.093	0.265	**0.726**
FSL2	−0.152	−0.051	0.114	0.105	0.140	0.084	**0.664**
FSL3	−0.170	−0.179	0.024	0.106	0.285	0.011	**0.585**
PL1	−0.074	−0.121	0.120	**0.626**	0.197	0.157	0.221
PL2	−0.165	−0.118	−0.036	**0.531**	0.362	0.238	−0.127
PL3	−0.218	−0.068	0.079	**0.717**	0.043	0.105	0.003
SCCL1	0.072	**0.737**	0.055	0.077	−0.101	−0.125	0.003
SCCL2	0.153	**0.764**	−0.065	−0.041	−0.193	−0.058	−0.104
SCCL3	0.204	**0.788**	−0.122	−0.029	−0.107	−0.025	−0.034
SCCL4	0.182	**0.731**	−0.040	−0.071	−0.116	−0.042	−0.113
SCCL5	0.206	**0.770**	0.024	−0.067	−0.061	0.037	−0.143
CI1	**0.668**	.217	−0.051	−0.200	0.030	−0.154	0.108
CI2	**0.766**	0.161	−0.114	−0.216	−0.121	−0.136	0.012
CI3	**0.807**	0.169	−0.112	−0.081	−0.119	−0.200	0.066
CI4	**0.791**	0.142	−0.128	−0.082	−0.114	−0.174	−0.121
CI5	**0.784**	0.136	0.001	−0.066	0.035	0.045	−0.139
CI6	**0.784**	0.081	−0.036	−0.006	−0.140	0.079	−0.241
SEB1	−0.089	−0.122	0.193	0.276	**0.634**	−0.183	0.166
SEB2	−0.062	−0.208	0.132	−0.003	**0.704**	0.187	0.225
SEB3	−0.183	−0.035	0.070	0.156	**0.727**	0.090	−0.003
SEB4	−0.140	0.081	−0.036	−0.006	**0.714**	0.079	−0.241
OE1	−0.212	0.093	**0.674**	−0.129	0.159	0.142	0.066

(continued)

(continued)

Items	Component						
	1	2	3	4	5	6	7
OE2	0.038	−0.017	**0.819**	0.013	0.071	−0.054	0.061
OE3	−0.090	0.006	**0.843**	0.168	0.090	0.043	−0.010
Eigen values	7.479	2.922	2.460	1.826	1.437	1.348	1.101
Percentage of variance explained	15.018	12.751	8.878	6.818	6.647	5.920	5.880
Cumulative % of variance explained	15.018	27.769	36.647	43.465	50.112	56.031	61.911
KMO and Bartlett's test of sphericity	KMO = 0.839, Bartlett's test of sphericity χ^2 (435) = 2982.412, $p < 0.001$						

Note SCL = Self-Centered Leadership, FSL = Face-Saving Leadership, PL = Procedural Leadership, SCCL = Status-Conscious Leadership, CI = Conflict Inducer Leadership, OE = Organizational Effectiveness, SEB = Strategic Entrepreneurial Behavior

Appendix 10: Exploratory Factor Analysis (Control Variables), Ghana

Items	Component			
	1	2	3	4
MD1	−0.072	**0.797**	0.030	−0.032
MD2	0.000	**0.790**	−0.139	−0.012
MD3	−0.063	**0.812**	−0.069	0.177
MD4	0.039	**0.781**	−0.053	0.179
TD1	**0.777**	−0.040	0.044	−0.027
TD2	**0.784**	−0.001	0.089	0.022
TD3	**0.678**	−0.074	0.101	0.149
TD4	**0.771**	0.006	0.116	−0.028
TD5	**0.607**	0.014	0.185	0.356
MU1	0.399	−0.030	0.077	**0.625**
MU2	−0.028	0.213	0.110	**0.691**
MU3	0.017	0.091	0.087	**0.701**
ED1	0.043	−0.055	**0.754**	−0.151
ED2	0.117	−0.126	**0.716**	−0.026
ED3	0.057	0.045	**0.648**	0.163
ED4	0.158	−0.053	**0.664**	0.356
ED5	0.209	−0.094	**0.635**	0.354
Eigen values	3.961	2.807	1.893	1.204
Percentage of variance explained	17.048	15.426	14.509	11.047
Cumulative % of variance explained	17.048	32.474	46.982	58.029
KMO and Bartlett's test of sphericity	KMO = 0.782, Bartlett's test of sphericity χ^2 (136) = 1210.938, $p < 0.001$			

Note MD = Market Dynamism, TD = Technological Dynamism, MU = Market Uncertainty, ED = Environmental Dynamism

Appendix 11: Confirmatory Factor Analysis (Main Variables), Kenya

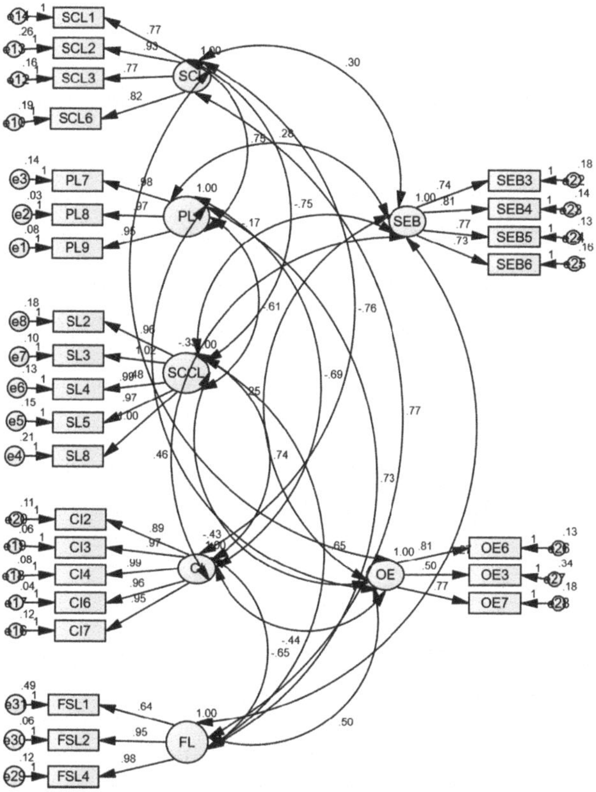

SCL = Self-Centered Leadership, FL = Face-Saving Leadership, PL = Procedural Leadership, SCCL = Status-Conscious Leadership, CI = Conflict Inducer Leadership, SEB = Strategic Entrepreneurial Behavior and OE = Organizational Effectiveness

Appendix 12: Confirmatory Factor Analysis (Control Variables), Kenya

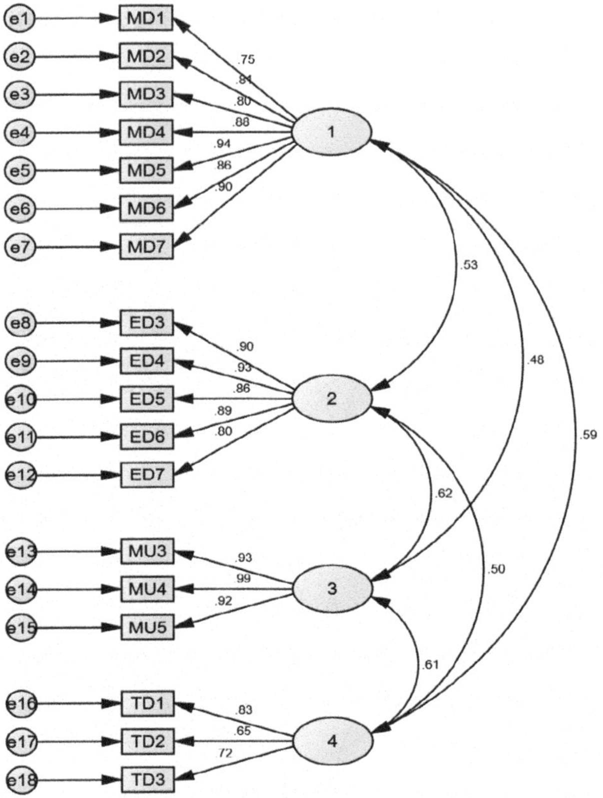

1 = Market Dynamism, 2 = Environmental Dynamism, MU = Market Uncertainty and TD = Technological Dynamism

Appendix 13: Confirmatory Factor Analysis (Main Variables), Ghana

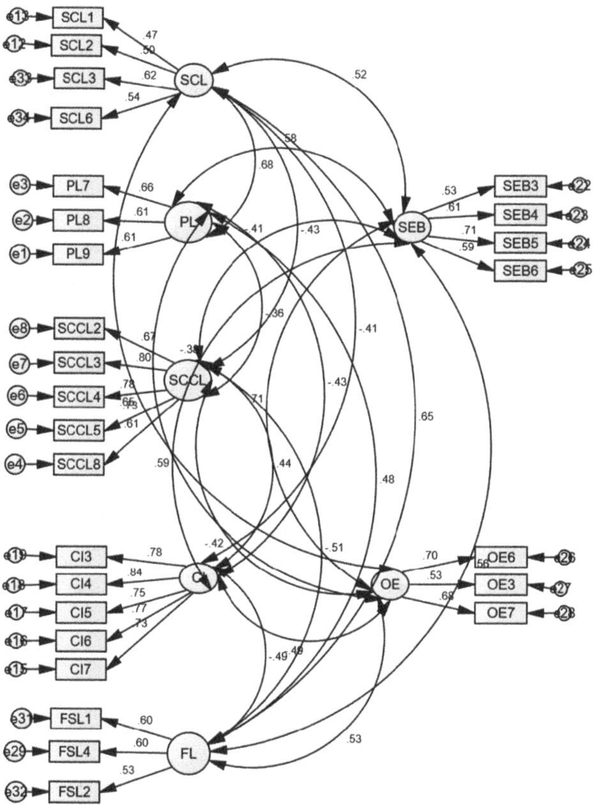

SCL = Self-Centered Leadership, FL = Face-Saving Leadership, PL = Procedural Leadership, SCCL = Status-Conscious Leadership, CI = Conflict Inducer Leadership, SEB = Strategic Entrepreneurial Behavior and OE = Organizational Effectiveness

Appendix 14: Confirmatory Factor Analysis (Control Variables), Ghana

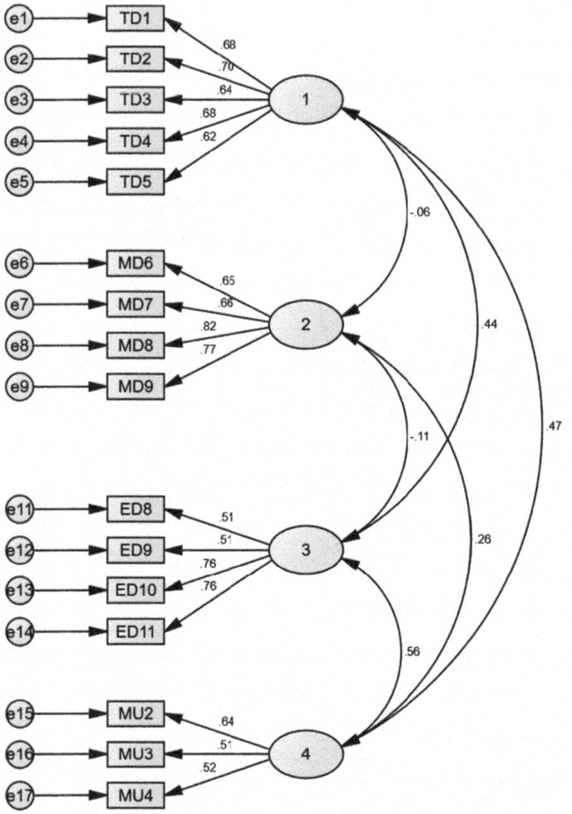

1 = Technological Dynamism, 2 = Market Dynamism, 3 = Environmental Dynamism and 4 = Market Uncertainty

Appendix 15: Confirmatory Factor Analysis (Main Variables), Kenya

*Model 1	Operational measures of construct Model Fit Indexes: $\chi^2 = 723.550$; d.f. = 303; χ^2/d.f. = 2.388; *RMSEA = 0.091; CFI = 0.909; IFI = 0.910; TLI = 0.900; SRMR = 0.057	λ	t-value	α	CR
Item labels					
	Conflict-Inducing			0.982	0.982
CI1	1. My CEO/MD reprimands without listening to employees	0.941	14.165		
CI2	2. My CEO/MD makes fun of employees and humiliates them	0.977	15.206		
CI3	3. My CEO/MD addresses employees in unprofessional terms, either at work or publicly	0.960	14.708		
CI4	4. My CEO/MD sometimes makes insulting or disrespectful remarks during the working hours toward employees	0.969	14.962		
CI5	5. My CEO/MD makes sexual remarks toward workers/flirts with them	0.937	14.080		
	Self-Centered Leadership			0.969	0.969
SCCL1	1. The business is always about the CEO/MD	0.910	13.320		
SCCL2	2. My CEO/MD does not involve others to participate in the decision process of the business	0.928	13.797		
SCCL3	3. My CEO/MD likes to do things alone where he/she works and acts separately from others	0.941	14.141		
SCCL4	4. My CEO/MD avoids people or groups and prefers his/her own company	0.954	14.493		

(continued)

(continued)

*Model 1	Operational measures of construct Model Fit Indexes: χ^2 = 723.550; d.f. = 303; χ^2/d.f. = 2.388; *RMSEA = 0.091; CFI = 0.909; IFI = 0.910; TLI = 0.900; SRMR = 0.057	λ	t-value	α	CR
SCCL5	5. My CEO/MD is always pursuing his/her own interest	0.913	13.415		
	Face-saving Leadership			0.896	0.904
FSL1	1. My CEO/MD protects his/her reputation in all circumstances	0.944	14.088		
FSL2	2. My CEO/MD shows humility and preserves harmony in his/her relationships	0.969	14.763		
FSL3	3. My CEO/MD acts defensively sometimes	0.677	8.575		
	Status-Conscious Leadership			0.919	0.922
SCL1	1. My CEO/MD approaches problems from different perspectives	0.884	12.529		
SCL2	2. My CEO/MD remains neutral in everyday decision-making	0.888	12.622		
SCL3	3. My CEO/MD collects information and learns from experience	0.875	12.333		
SCL4	4. My CEO/MD is clear in discussions	0.808	10.878		
	Procedural Leadership			0.971	0.972
PL1	1. My CEO/MD applies procedures consistently	0.960	14.688		
PL2	2. My CEO/MD applies processes free of bias	0.986	15.438		
PL3	3. My CEO/MD makes decisions based on facts	0.933	13.958		
	Organizational Effectiveness			0.852	0.859

(continued)

(continued)

	Operational measures of construct				
*Model 1	Model Fit Indexes: $\chi^2 = 723.550$; d.f. = 303; χ^2/d.f. = 2.388; *RMSEA = 0.091; CFI = 0.909; IFI = 0.910; TLI = 0.900; SRMR = 0.057	λ	t-value	α	CR
OE1	1. In general, the desired level of output is always attained by my firm	0.915	12.459		
OE2	2. In general, the needs and expectations of customers are often met	0.647	7.853		
OE3	3. In general, set targets of products/services are achieved at all times	0.877	11.729		
	Strategic Entrepreneurial Behavior			0.937	0.938
SEB1	1. In general, top managers of my firm prefer to lead our industry in new product introduction	0.868	12.160		
SEB2	2. In general, top managers of my firm have bias toward leading our industry into new product introductions	0.909	13.127		
SEB3	3. In general, my firm is the first to introduce new products in our industry	0.902	12.972		
SEB4	4. In general, top managers of my firm respond to competitors by introducing new product innovations	0.876	12.358		

Note All items were measured on five-point scales anchored by 1 = "strongly disagree" and 5 = "strongly agree"
λ = Standardized Factor Loadings, CR = Composite Reliability
*In Model 1, RMSEA = 0.091 above the expected threshold. But other relevant fit indices were within range

Appendix 16: Confirmatory Factor Analysis (Control Variables), Kenya

Model 2	Operational measures of construct Model Fit Indexes: $\chi^2 = 250.659$; d.f. = 121; χ^2/d.f. = 2.072; RMSEA = 0.059; CFI = 0.945; IFI = 0.946; TLI = 0.931; SRMR = 0.048	λ	t-value	α	CR
Item labels					
	Technological Dynamism			0.872	0.775
TD1	1. The technology in our industry is changing very rapidly	0.837	10.301		
TD2	2. Technological changes provide big opportunities in our industry	0.644	7.438		
TD3	3. A large number of new product ideas have been made possible through technological breakthroughs in our industry	0.706	8.326		
	Market Dynamics			0.946	0.950
MD1	1. In our firm, customer demand and product preferences change quite rapidly	0.768	10.158		
MD2	2. New customers tend to have product needs that are quite different from existing customers	0.827	11.784		
MD3	3. Our customers tend to look for new products all the times	0.829	11.533		
MD4	4. Customers tend to prefer our products to our competitors'	0.894	13.100		
MD5	5. Regarding our flagship product, our firm has the largest market share	0.933	13.858		
MD6	6. Regarding our flagship product, our firm has the smallest market share	0.851	11.829		

(continued)

(continued)

Model 2	Operational measures of construct Model Fit Indexes: $\chi^2 = 250.659$; d.f. = 121; χ^2/d.f. = 2.072; RMSEA = 0.059; CFI = 0.945; IFI = 0.946; TLI = 0.931; SRMR = 0.048	λ	t-value	α	CR
MD7	7. Regarding our flagship product, our firm has medical market share	0.869	12.257		
	Environmental Dynamism			0.943	0.940
ED1	1. Our business unit rarely changes its marketing practices to keep up with competitors	0.903	13.083		
ED2	2. The rate at which new product becomes obsolete in the industry is very slow	0.947	14.312		
ED3	3. Actions of competitors are quite easy to predict	0.859	12.274		
ED4	4. The set of competitors in my industry have remained the same	0.861	12.074		
ED5	5. Product demand is easy to forecast	0.775	10.129		
	Market Uncertainty			0.960	0.960
MU1	1. Customers' products/services preferences change rapidly	0.928	13.777		
MU2	2. Customers tend to look for new products at all times	0.988	15.567		
MU3	3. Demand is hard to forecast	0.912	13.548		

Note All items were measured on five-point scales anchored by 1 = "strongly disagree" and 5 = "strongly agree"
λ = Standardized Factor Loadings, CR = Composite Reliability

Appendix 17: Confirmatory Factor Analysis (Main Variables), Ghana

Model 1	Operational measures of construct Model Fit Indexes: $\chi^2 = 480.348$; d.f. = 303; χ^2/d.f. = 1.585; RMSEA = 0.050; CFI = 0.914; IFI = 0.915; TLI = 0.900; SRMR = 0.053	λ	t-value	α	CR
Item labels					
	Conflict-Inducing			0.891	0.883
CI1	1. My CEO/MD reprimands without listening to employees	0.729	16.338		
CI2	2. My CEO/MD makes fun of employees and humiliates them	0.774	15.744		
CI3	3. My CEO/MD addresses employees in unprofessional terms, either at work or publicly	0.750	12.013		
CI4	4. My CEO/MD sometimes makes insulting or disrespectful remarks during the working hours toward employees	0.837	11.467		
CI5	5. My CEO/MD makes sexual remarks toward workers/flirts with them	0.783	10.401		
	Self-Centered Leadership			0.639	0.614
SCCL1	1. The business is always about the CEO/MD	0.607	7.454		
SCCL2	2. My CEO/MD does not involve others to participate in the decision process of the business	0.735	7.302		
SCCL3	3. My CEO/MD likes to do things alone where he/she works and acts separately from others	0.777	7.422		
SCCL4	4. My CEO/MD avoids people or groups and prefers his/her own company	0.801	12.308		

(continued)

(continued)

Model 1	Operational measures of construct Model Fit Indexes: $\chi^2 = 480.348$; d.f. = 303; $\chi^2/$d.f. = 1.585; RMSEA = 0.050; CFI = 0.914; IFI = 0.915; TLI = 0.900; SRMR = 0.053	λ	t-value	α	CR
SCCL5	5. My CEO/MD is always pursuing his/her own interest	0.671	13.302		
	Face-Saving Leadership			0.600	0.601
FSL1	1. My CEO/MD protects his/her reputation in all circumstances	0.605	7.889		
FSL2	2. My CEO/MD shows humility and preserves harmony in his/her relationships	0.596	7.248		
FSL3	3. My CEO/MD acts defensively sometimes	0.534	8.195		
	Status-Conscious Leadership			0.780	0.843
SCL1	1. My CEO/MD approaches problems from different perspectives	0.504	10.640		
SCL2	2. My CEO/MD remains neutral in everyday decision-making	0.500	13.474		
SCL3	3. My CEO/MD collects information and learns from experience	0.618	13.710		
SCL4	4. My CEO/MD is clear in discussions	0.514	12.688		
	Procedural Leadership			0.700	0.700
PL1	1. My CEO/MD applies procedures consistently	0.606	9.499		
PL2	2. My CEO/MD applies processes free of bias	0.608	8.440		
PL3	3. My CEO/MD makes decisions based on facts	0.659	8.535		
				0.700	0.700
	Organizational Effectiveness			0.700	0.701
OE1	1. In general, the desired level of output is always attained by my firm	0.699	7.761		

(continued)

(continued)

Model 1	Operational measures of construct Model Fit Indexes: $\chi^2 = 480.348$; d.f. = 303; $\chi^2/$d.f. = 1.585; RMSEA = 0.050; CFI = 0.914; IFI = 0.915; TLI = 0.900; SRMR = 0.053	λ	t-value	α	CR
OE2	2. In general, the needs and expectations of customers are often met	0.530	15.344		
OE3	3. In general, set targets of products/services are achieved at all times	0.682	12.436		
	Strategic Entrepreneurial Behavior			0.700	0.704
SEB1	1. In general, top managers of my firm prefer to lead our industry in new product introduction	0.527	7.618		
SEB2	2. In general, top managers of my firm have bias toward leading our industry into new product introductions	0.611	9.469		
SEB3	3. In general, my firm is the first to introduce new products in our industry	0.705	9.060		
SEB4	4. In general, top managers of my firm respond to competitors by introducing new product innovations	0.594	8.989		

Note All items were measured on five-point scales anchored by 1 = "strongly disagree" and 5 = "strongly agree"
λ = Standardized Factor Loadings, CR = Composite Reliability.

Appendix 18: Confirmatory Factor Analysis (Control Variables), Ghana

Model 2	Model Fit Indexes: χ^2 = 178.068; d.f = 98; χ^2/d.f. = 1.817; RMSEA = 0.059; CFI = 0.922; IFI = 0.924; TLI = 0.904; SRMR = 0.070	λ	t-value	α	CR
Item labels					
	Technological Dynamism			0.791	0.798
TD1	1. The technology in our industry is changing very rapidly	0.678	10.631		
TD2	2. Technological changes provide big opportunities in our industry	0.704	11.147		
TD3	3. A large number of new product ideas have been made possible through technological breakthroughs in our industry	0.640	9.879		
TD4	4. There have been major technological developments in our industry	0.680	10.668		
TD5	5. Our firm invests in technological training to drive the business	0.621	9.520		
	Market Dynamics			0.816	0.815
MD1	1. In our firm, customer demand and product preferences change quite rapidly	0.648	10.203		
MD2	2. New customers tend to have product needs that are quite different from existing customers	0.658	10.399		
MD3	3. Our customers tend to look for new products all the times	0.816	13.636		
MD4	4. Customers tend to prefer our products to our competitors'	0.768	12.636		
	Environmental Dynamism			0.726	0.732

(continued)

(continued)

Model 2	Model Fit Indexes: χ^2 = 178.068; d.f = 98; χ^2/d.f. = 1.817; RMSEA = 0.059; CFI = 0.922; IFI = 0.924; TLI = 0.904; SRMR = 0.070	λ	t-value	α	CR
ED1	1. Our business unit rarely changes its marketing practices to keep up with competitors	0.512	7.466		
ED2	2. The rate at which new product becomes obsolete in the industry is very slow	0.514	7.497		
ED3	3. Actions of competitors are quite easy to predict	0.758	11.736		
ED4	4. The set of competitors in my industry have remained the same	0.758	11.734		
	Market Uncertainty			0.568	0.572
MU1	1. Customers' products/services preferences change rapidly	0.640	8.259		
MU2	2. Customers tend to look for new products at all times	0.510	6.660		
MU3	3. Demand is hard to forecast	0.517	6.752		

Note All items were measured on five-point scales anchored by 1 = "strongly disagree" and 5 = "strongly agree"
λ = Standardized Factor Loadings, CR = Composite Reliability

Appendix 19: Correlation Among Variables and Validity, Kenya

Variables	1	2	3	4	5	6	7	8	9	10	11
1. Market Dynamism	**0.943**										
2. Technology Dynamism	0.599**	**0.871**									
3. Market Uncertainty	0.489**	0.495**	**0.854**								
4. Environmental Dynamism	0.496**	0.396**	0.499**	**0.733**							
5. Self-Centered	−0.417**	−0.342**	−0.394**	−0.420**	**0.929**						
6. Self-Conscious	−0.538**	−0.378**	-0.363**	−0.407**	0.504**	**0.864**					
7. Conflict Inducer	−0.606**	−0.411**	-0.480**	−0.451**	0.616**	0.745**	**0.957**				
8. Face-Saving	0.568**	0.413**	0.435**	0.470**	−0.678**	−0.575**	−0.626**	**0.874**			
9. Procedural	0.477**	0.410**	0.400**	0.496**	−0.635**	−0.638**	−0.709**	0.656**	**0.960**		
10. Strategic Entrepreneurial Behavior (SEB)	0.458**	0.452**	0.557**	0.405**	−0.210*	−0.131	−0.306**	0.306**	0.246**	**0.889**	
11. Organizational Effectiveness	0.532**	0.535**	0.391**	0.355**	−0.370**	−0.363**	−0.497**	0.514**	0.503**	0.428**	**0.822**

(continued)

Variables	1	2	3	4	5	6	7	8	9	10	11
Mean	5.047	3.681	3.452	3.260	3.948	2.094	1.846	4.033	4.055	3.271	5.047
Standard deviation	0.869	0.861	0.712	0.638	0.841	0.994	0.963	0.890	0.974	0.770	1.300
Skewness	−1.188	−0.463	−0.097	−0.550	−1.189	0.960	1.152	−1.332	−1.284	−0.038	-1.033
Kurtosis	1.342	−0.179	−0.146	1.447	0.951	0.183	0.651	2.005	1.173	0.141	0.646
AVE	**0.890**	**0.758**	**0.730**	**0.538**	**0.864**	**0.747**	**0.916**	**0.764**	**0.922**	**0.790**	**0.675**

$^{**}p < 0.01$, $^{***}p < 0.001$ (two-tailed)
AVE = Average Variance Extracted
The squared root of the AVE is presented diagonally in bold

Appendix 20: Correlation Among Variables and Validity, Ghana

Variables	1	2	3	4	5	6	7	8	9	10	11
1. Market Dynamism	**0.727**										
2. Technology Dynamism	0.334**	**0.700**									
3. Market Uncertainty	0.204**	−0.107	**0.700**								
4. Environmental Dynamism	0.290**	0.347**	−0.051	**0.700**							
5. Self-Centered	0.141*	−0.198**	.449**	−0.385**	**0.730**						
6. Self-Conscious	0.123	0.213**	−0.211**	0.270**	−0.242**	**0.700**					
7. Conflict Inducer	−0.166*	−0.265**	0.233**	−0.327**	0.387**	−0.317**	**0.752**				
8. Face-Saving	0.179**	0.297**	−0.216**	0.393**	−0.347**	0.348**	−0.341**	**0.700**			
9. Procedural	0.208**	0.407**	−0.203**	0.441**	−0.247**	0.372**	−0.363**	0.290**	**0.700**		
10. Strategic Entrepreneurial Behavior (SEB)	0.161*	0.418**	−0.175**	0.388**	−0.282**	0.250**	−0.314**	0.350**	0.390**	**0.700**	
11. Organizational Effectiveness	0.168**	0.340**	−0.026	0.248**	−0.049	0.192**	−0.189**	0.193**	0.184**	0.290**	**0.718**

(continued)

Variables	1	2	3	4	5	6	7	8	9	10	11
Mean	3.567	3.676	3.129	3.923	3.060	3.915	2.558	4.067	3.932	3.813	5.159
Standard deviation	0.687	0.672	0.924	0.630	0.929	0.673	1.011	0.631	0.645	0.709	0.999
Skewness	−0.215	−0.312	−0.312	−0.306	−0.798	−0.66	−0.022	−1.018	−0.704	−0.468	−0.219
Kurtosis	0.393	1.522	−0.157	1.447	0.017	1.133	−0.957	3.794	2.147	1.003	0.799
AVE	**0.527**	**0.500**	**0.500**	**0.500**	**0.534**	**0.500**	**0.565**	**0.500**	**0.500**	**0.500**	**0.516**

** $p < 0.01$, *** $p < 0.001$ (two-tailed)
AVE = Average Variance Extracted
The squared root of the AVE is presented diagonally in bold

Appendix 21: Regression Analysis of Measured Variables

Variables	Kenya sample				Ghana sample			
	Model 1 β (*t*-values)	Model 2 β (*t*-values)	Model 3 β (*t*-values)	Model 4 β (*t*-values)	Model 1 β (*t*-values)	Model 2 β (*t*-values)	Model 3 β (*t*-values)	Model 4 β (*t*-values)
Control Variables								
Market Dynamism	0.098 (1.092)	−0.009 (−0.099)	−0.026 (-0.259)	−0.017 (0.180)	00.61 (0.888)	0.061 (0.877)	0.034 (0.485)	−0.013 (-0.182)
Technology Dynamism	0.073 (0.814)	0.046 (0.515)	0.043 (0.0482)	0.023 (0.267)	−0.078 (1.160)	0.027 (0.367)	−0.003 (-0.036)	−0.029 (-0.401)
Market uncertainty	0.080 (0.954)	0.028 (0.335)	0.026 (0.310)	−0.060 (-0.729)	0.079 (1.165)	0.030 (0.402)	0.040 (0.549)	0.021 (0.305)
Environmental Dynamism	0.525 (7.400)***	0.521 (7.489)***	0.516 (7.320)***	0.516 (7.892)***	0.176 (2.668)**	0.184 (2.739)**	0.157 (2.353)**	0.173 (2.650)**
Independent Variables								
Self-Centered Leadership		0.234 (1.509)	0.251 (1.581)	1.168 (2.566)		0.019 (0.231)	0.022 (0.272)	−0.994 (−2.610)**
Self-Conscious Leadership		−0.079 (−0.741)	-0.089 (−0.816)	0.282 (0.632)		0.116 (0.864)	0.100 (0.754)	0.277 (0.334)
Conflict Inducer Leadership		−0.022 (-0.189)	−0.061 (−0.141)	−0.744 (−1.573)		−0.025 (−0.353)	−0.011 (−0.155)	−0.953 (−1.844)+
Face-Saving Leadership		0.060 (0.595)	0.059 (0.587)	0.279 (0.610)		−0.003 (−0.036)	−0.024 (−0.303)	−0.079 (−0.179)
Procedural Leadership		−0.112 (−1.042)	−0.112 (−1.041)	−1.678 (−4.168)***		0.069 (0.891)	0.032 (0.411)	−1.174 (−2.791)**
Moderator								
SEB			0.045 (0.538)	−0.026 (−0.033)			0.195 (2.604)**	−2.654 (−4.023)***
Interaction Effect								

(continued)

(continued)

Variables	Kenya sample Model 1 β (*t*-values)	Kenya sample Model 2 β (*t*-values)	Kenya sample Model 3 β (*t*-values)	Kenya sample Model 4 β (*t*-values)	Ghana sample Model 1 β (*t*-values)	Ghana sample Model 2 β (*t*-values)	Ghana sample Model 3 β (*t*-values)	Ghana sample Model 4 β (*t*-values)
Self-Centered × SEB				1.600 (2.070)*				1.796 (2.716)**
Self-Conscious × SEB				−0.381 (−0.816)				−0.451 (−0.271)
Conflict Inducer × SEB				0.651 (1.473)				0.990 (1.913)+
Face-Saving × SEB				−0.284 (−0.369)				0.047 (0.060)
Procedural × SEB				2.529 (4.025)***				2.016 (2.777)***
R^2	0.443	0.510	0.511	0.607	0.110	0.130	0.156	0.267
Adjusted R^2	0.420	0.463	0.460	0.542	0.086	0.083	0.107	0.267
F value	19.404***	10.961***	10.010***	9.353***	4.678***	2.773***	3.148***	3.148***
ΔR^2		0.067	0.001	0.096		0.130	0.156	0.06
Partial *F* value		2.630*	0.290	4.443***		2.112*	3.190***	4.234***
Degrees of freedom	4/123	9/118	10/119	15/112	4/230	9/225	10/224	15/219

Significance level = $^+p < 0.05$, $^*p < 0.05$, $^{**}p < 0.01$, $^{***}p < 0.001$

Note Standardized regression coefficients were reported with *t*-values for each effect in parentheses

Appendix 22: ANOVA Representation of Measured Outputs

Variables	Kenya		Ghana		t test	
	Mean	SD	Mean	SD	*t*	*p*-value
1. Self-Centered Leadership	3.83	0.853	3.22	0.528	−7.455	0.000
2. Self-Conscious Leadership	2.63	1.220	3.80	0.585	10.511	0.000
3. Conflict Inducer Leadership	2.02	1.052	2.90	0.744	8.441	0.000
4. Face-saving Leadership	3.99	0.857	4.00	0.447	0.164	0.870
5. Procedural Leadership	4.01	0.935	3.77	0.464	−2.718	0.007
6. Organizational Effectiveness	3.92	0.728	3.56	0.518	−5.06	0.000

Appendix 23: Interaction Plots, Kenya

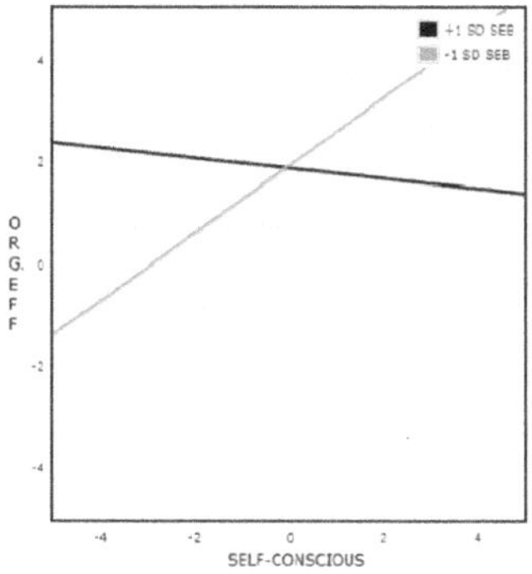

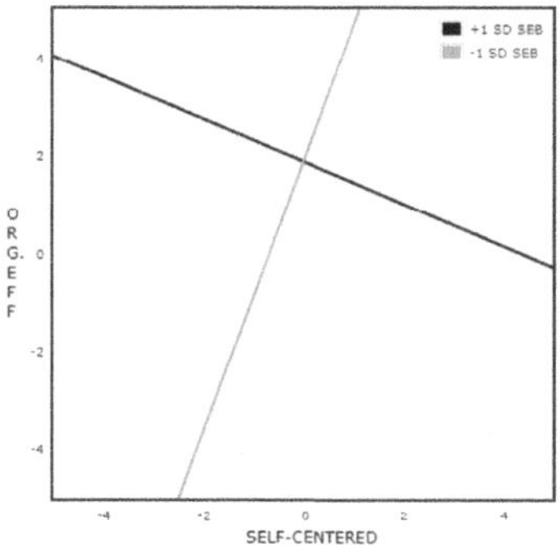

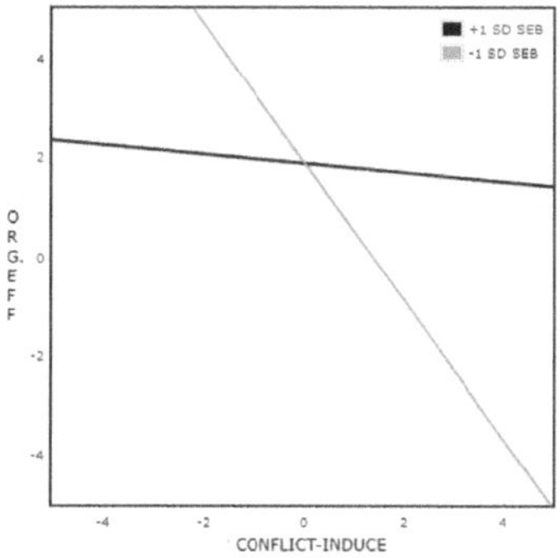

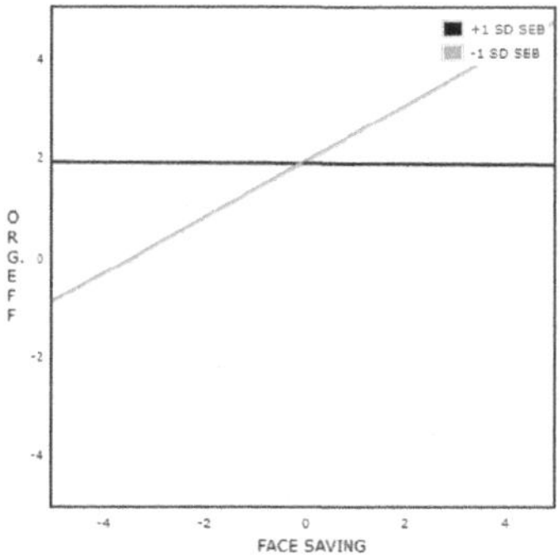

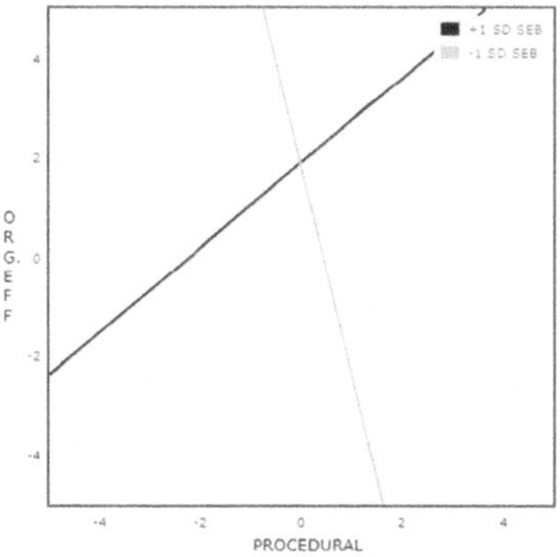

Appendix 24: Interaction Plots, Ghana

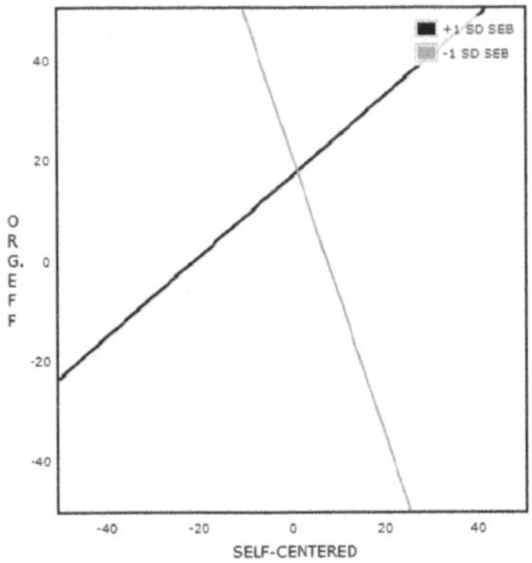

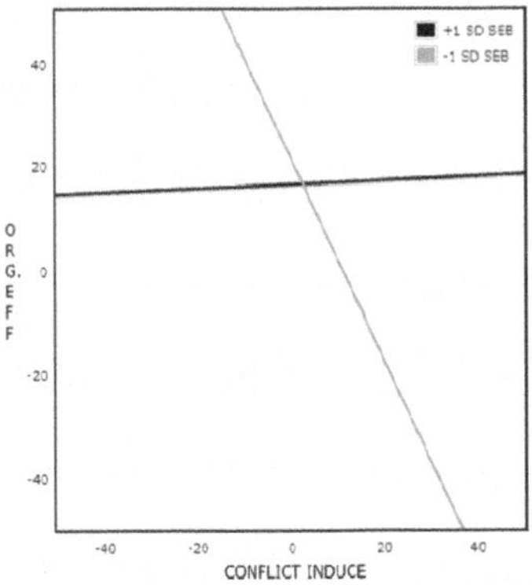

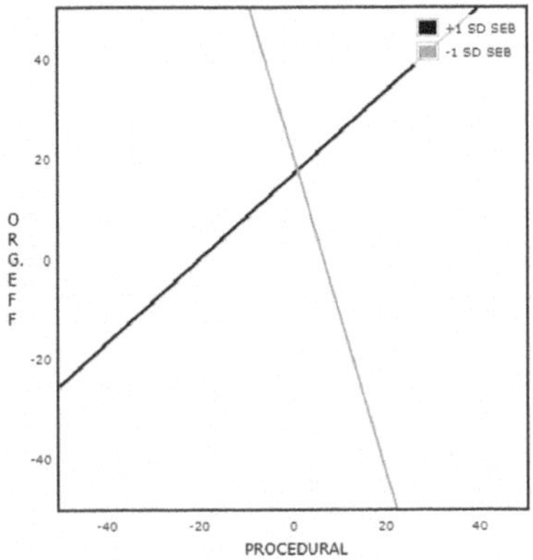

Appendix 25: Profile of Case Study Interviewees

Respondent	Position/occupation	Years of experience	Qualification/area of expertise	Interview duration	Venue of interview
Industry expert	Professor of Marketing communication	30 years	Academia	23 minutes	In-person, office
Industry expert	Former President, AAG	40 years	Advertising agency	27 minutes	In-person, office
Industry expert	AAG Secretariat	10 years	Industry experience and supervision	31 minutes	Via phone call
Business owner/ founder	CEO	42 years	Advertising agency	18 minutes	In-person, office
Business owner/ founder	Managing Director	26 years	Marketing practitioner	25 minutes	In-person, office
Business owner/ founder	Managing Director	30 years	Engineering background	33 minutes	Via phone call
Business owner/ founder	Managing Director	18 years	Marketing background	21 minutes	In-person, office
Business owner/ founder	CEO	10 years	Social scientist	23 minutes	Via phone call
Business leader	CEO	8 years	Finance background	27 minutes	Via phone call
Business leader	CEO	13 years	Architectural background	24 minutes	Via phone call
Business leader	COO	31 years	Below the line marketing expert	30 minutes	In-person, office
Business leader	Production Manager	15 years	Below the line marketing expert	31 minutes	In-person, office
Business leader	Production Manager	31 years	Marketing expert	26 minutes	Via Phone Call

Appendix 26: Questionnaire Instrument

Section A

Please Indicate (by ticking) the extent to which you agree with the following statements concerning the leadership behavior of your CEO/MD.

(*1 = "Strongly Disagree," 2 = "Disagree," 3 = "Indifferent," 4 = "Agree," 5 = "Strongly Agree"*)

S/N	Status-Conscious Leadership	1	2	3	4	5
1	My CEO/MD approaches problems from different perspectives	1	2	3	4	5
2	My CEO/MD remains neutral in everyday decision-making	1	2	3	4	5
3	My CEO/MD collects information and learns from experience	1	2	3	4	5
4	My CEO/MD is clear in discussions	1	2	3	4	5
5	My CEO/MD is able to assume responsibility	1	2	3	4	5
6	My CEO/MD communicates fairly and openly	1	2	3	4	5
7	My CEO/MD aims toward positive outcomes	1	2	3	4	5
8	My CEO/MD promotes and builds on collective conscious of staff	1	2	3	4	5
9	My CEO/MD monitors activities keenly	1	2	3	4	5

S/N	Face-Saving Leadership	1	2	3	4	5
1	My CEO/MD protects his/her reputation in all circumstances	1	2	3	4	5
2	My CEO/MD shows humility and preserves harmony in his/her relationships	1	2	3	4	5
3	My CEO/MD acts defensively sometimes	1	2	3	4	5
4	My CEO/MD avoids conflict when he/she speaks	1	2	3	4	5

S/N	Procedural Leadership	1	2	3	4	5
1	My CEO/MD applies procedures consistently	1	2	3	4	5
2	My CEO/MD applies processes free of bias	1	2	3	4	5

(continued)

(continued)

S/N	Procedural Leadership	1	2	3	4	5
3	My CEO/MD makes decisions based on facts	1	2	3	4	5
4	My CEO/MD upholds ethical and moral standards	1	2	3	4	5
5	My CEO/MD encourages employees to appeal decisions	1	2	3	4	5
6	My CEO/MD allows employees to voice out their opinion during meetings	1	2	3	4	5
7	My CEO/MD operates an open-door policy and is easily accessible	1	2	3	4	5
8	My CEO/MD encourages collaborative work relations at work and with clients	1	2	3	4	5
9	My CEO/MD encourages occasional updating of procedures	1	2	3	4	5

S/N	Self-Centered Leadership	1	2	3	4	5
1	The business is always about the CEO/MD	1	2	3	4	5
2	My CEO/MD does not involve others to participate in the decision process of the business	1	2	3	4	5
3	My CEO/MD likes to do things alone where he/she works and acts separately from others	1	2	3	4	5
4	My CEO/MD avoids people or groups and prefers his/her own company	1	2	3	4	5
5	My CEO/MD is always pursuing his/her own interest	1	2	3	4	5
6	My CEO/MD does not have a deputy or disregards the contribution of his/her deputy	1	2	3	4	5
7	My CEO/MD stifles worker initiatives	1	2	3	4	5
8	My CEO/MD sacrifices the workers' welfare to satisfy his/her own comforts	1	2	3	4	5

S/N	Conflict-Inducing	1	2	3	4	5
1	My CEO/MD reprimands without listening to employees	1	2	3	4	5
2	My CEO/MD makes fun of employees and humiliates them	1	2	3	4	5
3	My CEO/MD addresses employees in unprofessional terms, either at work or publicly	1	2	3	4	5
4	My CEO/MD sometimes makes insulting or disrespectful remarks during the working hours toward employees	1	2	3	4	5

(continued)

(continued)

S/N	Conflict-Inducing	1	2	3	4	5
6	My CEO/MD makes sexual remarks toward workers/ flirts with them	1	2	3	4	5
7	When my CEO/MD is mad at a worker, s/he punishes all employees	1	2	3	4	5
8	My CEO/MD exhibits rude behavior	1	2	3	4	5
9	My CEO/MD is disrespectful to clients	1	2	3	4	5

Section B

(1 = "Strongly Disagree," 2 = "Disagree," 3 = "Indifferent," 4 = "Agree," 5 = "Strongly Agree")

S/N	Strategic Entrepreneurial Behavior	1	2	3	4	5
1	In general, top managers of my firm prefer to lead our industry in new product introduction	1	2	3	4	5
2	In general, top managers of my firm have bias toward leading our industry into new product introductions	1	2	3	4	5
3	In general, my firm is the first to introduce new products in our industry	1	2	3	4	5
4	In general, top managers of my firm respond to competitors by introducing new product innovations	1	2	3	4	5
5	In general, top managers of my firm prefer to be ahead of the competition when introducing new products	1	2	3	4	5
6	In general, my firm commits resources toward researching the market and developing new products new based on the market insights	1	2	3	4	5

Section C

(1 = "Strongly Disagree," 2 = "Disagree," 3 = "Indifferent," 4 = "Agree," 5 = "Strongly Agree")

S/N	Organizational Effectiveness	1	2	3	4	5
1	In general, the desired level of output is always attained by my firm	1	2	3	4	5
2	In general, the needs and expectations of customers are often met	1	2	3	4	5
3	In general, set targets of products/services are achieved at all times	1	2	3	4	5
4	In general, production/services processes are regularly carried out efficiently	1	2	3	4	5
5	In general, desired market share is often attained	1	2	3	4	5
6	In general, standards of the regulatory agencies are regularly attained	1	2	3	4	5
7	In general, outputs/services are rendered within the shortest possible time	1	2	3	4	5

Section D

(1 = "Strongly Disagree," 2 = "Disagree," 3 = "Indifferent," 4 = "Agree," 5 = "Strongly Agree")

Control Variables

S/N	Market Dynamics	1	2	3	4	5
1	In our firm, customer demand and product preferences change quite rapidly	1	2	3	4	5
2	New customers tend to have product needs that are quite different from existing customers	1	2	3	4	5
3	Our customers tend to look for new products all the times	1	2	3	4	5
4	Customers tend to prefer our products to our competitors'	1	2	3	4	5
5	Regarding our flagship product, our firm has the largest market share	1	2	3	4	5
6	Regarding our flagship product, our firm has the smallest market share	1	2	3	4	5

(continued)

(continued)

S/N	Market Dynamics	1	2	3	4	5
7	Regarding our flagship product, our firm has medical market share	1	2	3	4	5
8	Regarding our flagship product, our firm has no market share	1	2	3	4	5
9	Regarding our flagship product, our firm is not aware of its market share	1	2	3	4	5

S/N	Technological Dynamism	1	2	3	4	5
1	The technology in our industry is changing very rapidly	1	2	3	4	5
2	Technological changes provide big opportunities in our industry	1	2	3	4	5
3	A large number of new product ideas have been made possible through technological breakthroughs in our industry	1	2	3	4	5
4	There have been major technological developments in our industry	1	2	3	4	5
5	Our firm invests in technological training to drive the business	1	2	3	4	5

S/N	Market Uncertainty	1	2	3	4	5
1	Customers' products/services preferences change rapidly	1	2	3	4	5
2	Customers tend to look for new products at all times	1	2	3	4	5
3	Demand is hard to forecast	1	2	3	4	5
4	New customers tend to have product-related needs that are different from those of existing customers	1	2	3	4	5
5	Customers demand products that do not yet exist in our local market	1	2	3	4	5

S/N	Environmental Dynamism	1	2	3	4	5
1	Our business unit rarely changes its marketing practices to keep up with competitors	1	2	3	4	5
2	The rate at which new product becomes obsolete in the industry is very slow	1	2	3	4	5
3	Actions of competitors are quite easy to predict	1	2	3	4	5

(continued)

(continued)

S/N	Environmental Dynamism	1	2	3	4	5
4	The set of competitors in my industry have remained the same	1	2	3	4	5
5	Product demand is easy to forecast	1	2	3	4	5
6	Customer's requirement/preferences are easy to forecast	1	2	3	4	5
7	Our business promotes the corporate brand	1	2	3	4	5
8	Our business promotes its products	1	2	3	4	5
9	Our competitors look to us before they make a move in the market	1	2	3	4	5
10	Compared with our competitors', our company's share of mindshare (the recall rate in consumers' mind) is optimum	1	2	3	4	5
11	Compared with our competitor', our company's share of voice (our share in the total advertising/marketing effort for the industry) is optimum	1	2	3	4	5

Section E

Demographic Information

1. Gender [ ] Male [ ] Female
2. Age [ ] 18–30 years [ ] 31–40 years [ ] 41–50 years [ ] 51–60 years [ ] 61 and above
3. What is your highest level of education? [ ] HND [ ] Bachelors [ ] Masters [ ] PhD/DBA [ ] Others, please specify________
4. What is your country of residence? [ ] Ghana [ ] Kenya
5. What is your current position in your company?
   [ ] Administrative officer [ ] Business unit [ ] Finance Officer [ ] Operating Officer
   [ ] CEO [ ] MD [ ] Business Owner Others. Please specify_
   ____
6. Please indicate the number of years your company has been in operation
   [ ] Below 1 year [ ] 1–2 years [ ] 2–3years
   [ ] 3–4 years [ ] 4–5 years [ ] 5 years and above

7. How many years have you worked in your organization?
   Less than 2 years [ ] 2–3 years [ ] 4 years and above [ ]
8. Please state your Return on Investment (ROI) of the last 2 years. E.g., GHS 20,000 ROI (refers the ratio) between net profit and cost of investment. Please state here ______________________________________.
9. To what extent are you confident about your knowledge of the issues in this questionnaire? Please note that 1 = Very little extent, 2 = little extent, 3 = moderate, 4 = large extent and 5 = very large extent

   Responses: 1 2 3 4 5

   Thank You for Your Time and Cooperation

Appendix 27: Case Study Interview Guide

a. Information about the researcher and the interview: **Time................................ Date.......................Venue ....**
b. Interviewer's Name...
c. Respondent's Name...
d. **Introduction:** The researcher is a student pursuing a doctoral degree in Business Leadership at Nobel International Business School (NiBS), an affiliate to SBS Swiss Business School in Zurich, Switzerland. Examining the above topic, the researcher is grateful to you for your committed time to this interview.
e. **Purpose of the research:** Please note that this study is purely for academic purposes and the questions are just eliciting your experience on the stated topic.
f. **Format for the interview:** The interview will not be more than 20 minutes.
g. **Consent and confidentiality of the respondent:** You are assured that whatever you share with me will be treated with utmost confidentiality and anonymity.

h. **Permission for audio recording:** With your permission, I will like to record our interview to enable me note all your comments without getting distracted by writing notes. Please note that the data generated from this interview will solely be for academic purposes and the responses generated henceforth shall be treated with the utmost confidentiality.

i. **Qualitative research objective:** To explore the challenges and opportunities of self-protective leadership.

j. **Interview questions**

1. What is the mindset of a self-protective leader?
2. What are the benefits of being a self-protective leader?
3. How does this leadership style affect the effectiveness of your firm?
4. What are some of the challenges associated with this leadership style in your firm?
5. How do you manage these challenges as a leader?
6. Are you familiar with procedural, self-centered, conflict inducing, status questions and face-saving sub-leadership traits?
7. Kindly share with me your experiences and opportunities associated with the self-protective leadership dimensions on start-up firms' effectiveness?

g. **Closing remarks**: Thank you for your time and participation. Again, you are assured of your outmost confidentiality. I will also be pleased if you will available for a follow-up interview? Do you also have any questions for me?

Index

D. K. Amoo-Osae, Jr, *Self-Protective Leadership and Organizational Effectiveness*, Palgrave Studies in African Leadership, https://doi.org/10.1007/978-3-031-61308-1

SPRINGER NATURE

GPSR Compliance

The European Union's (EU) General Product Safety Regulation (GPSR) is a set of rules that requires consumer products to be safe and our obligations to ensure this.

If you have any concerns about our products, you can contact us on ProductSafety@springernature.com

In case Publisher is established outside the EU, the EU authorized representative is:

Springer Nature Customer Service Center GmbH
Europaplatz 3
69115 Heidelberg, Germany

The manufacturer's authorised representative in the EU is Springer Nature Customer Service Centre GmbH, Europaplatz 3, 69115 Heidelberg, Germany. If you have any concerns regarding our products, please contact ProductSafety@springernature.com

Printed and bound by CPI Group (UK) Ltd, Croydon, CR0 4YY

01/10/2026

02225967-0004